122 Days

122 Days

a conversation in drawings & sentences

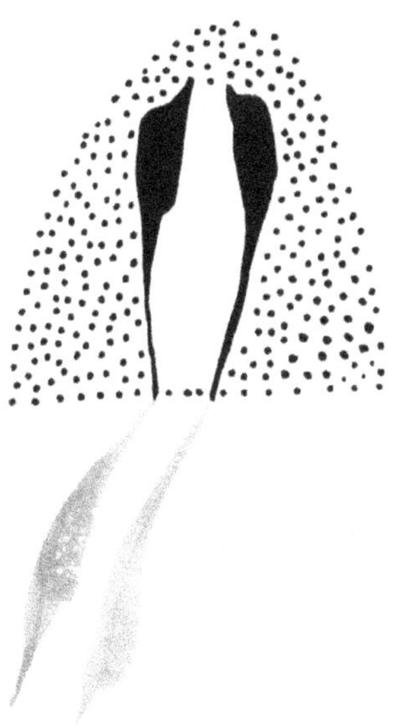

drawings by Angela Rose • sentences by Mary Kane

One Bird Books • Hatchville, Mass.

Very special thanks to Terre McNulty,
Jim Morgan, Annie Dean,
Dominic Arizona Bonuccelli,
Marilyn Robinson, and Dan Goers

ISBN: 979-8-9898147-0-1

One Bird Books
35 Brush Hill Road
Hatchville, MA 02536
www.onebirdbooks.com
onebirdbooks@gmail.com

One drawing. One sentence. One day. Those were the initial rules of the game. It started when an accident in the summer of 2019 left Angela unable to walk or work. She found herself isolated and unable to sculpt or practice performance art. So she decided to make a drawing. On a whim, she took a picture of the drawing and sent it, via text and without explanation, to me, a writer she'd met months earlier in a small artists' group. She saw it as a kind of SOS. Receiving the message, I went for a walk, thought about the drawing, and decided I'd like to write a sentence in response, which I did, and sent via text back to Angela.

From this exchange, we decided to keep going for a week, with only a few basic rules. First, there could be no judgments, no "I love it" or "I like it," no commentary whatsoever. In fact, other than exchanging sentences and drawings, we didn't communicate with each other. Second, the practice would occur daily, one drawing, one sentence. Either of us could work on our piece for as long as we wished on that day, but, finished or not, satisfied or not, at some point we had to press send.

After a week, we decided to try for another
week. And after that, we just kept going. In the
weeks that followed, we lived our daily lives with
one addition, the shared daily practice of this
absolutely private correspondence, not intended
as a finished piece or for public consumption.
But then, months later, after showing it to a few
friends, we decided that the work was worth
sharing.

122 Days is the record of that silent
conversation.

- Mary

To Aureleo Rosano (1939-2023)

122 Days

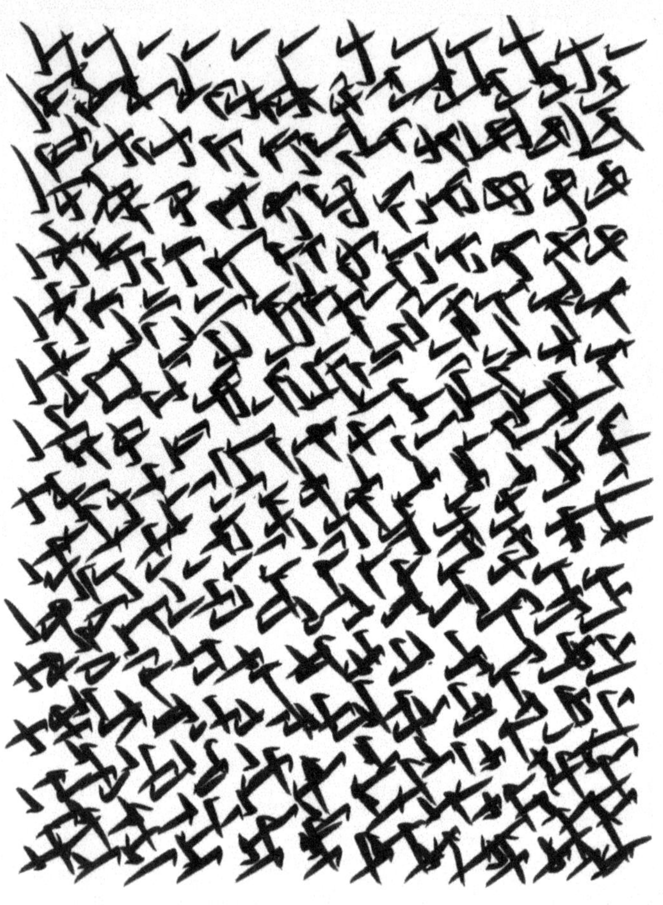

#1: Eleanor was always reading, reading, reading —reading a book in bed, reading the tone in a lover's comment, reading 127 swallows written on a blue morning.

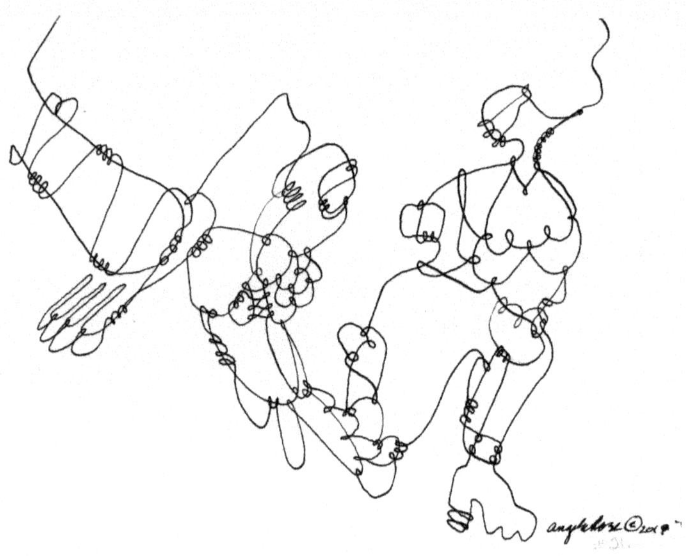

4

#2: So many parts of her self seemed inclined to
fly off, she thought, the very container of her
being threatened to become unrecognizable
(even to herself).

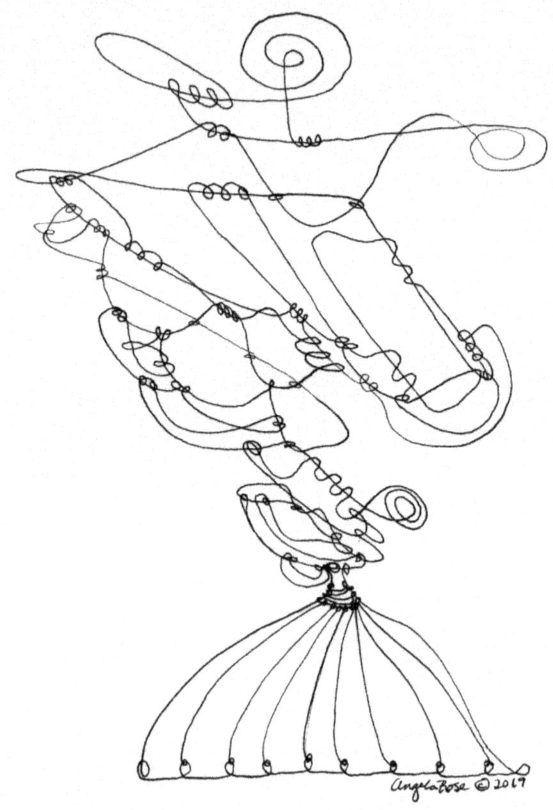

#3: She thought she might accept invitations to lecture extemporaneously.

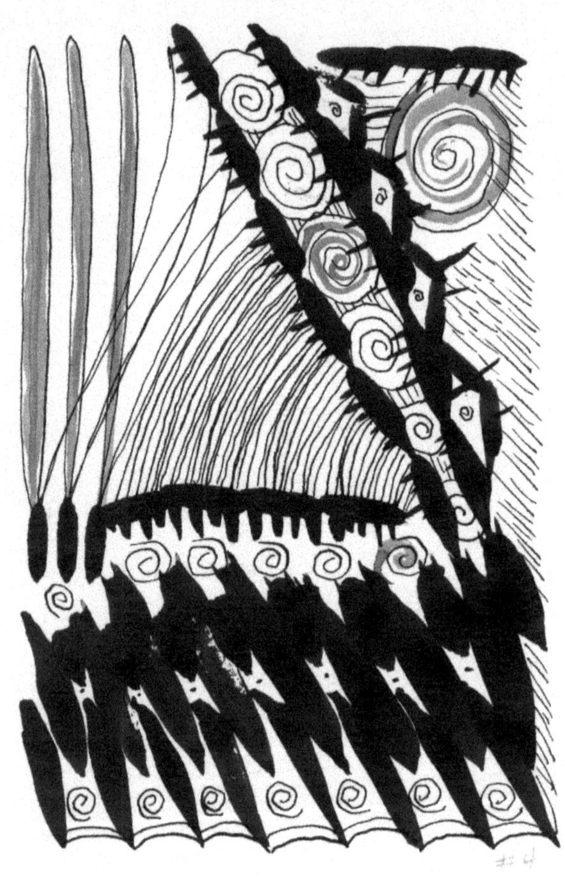

#4: She dipped her pen, and alas, what poured forth—mountains and rainclouds and sacred texts, specters and spirit guides, and, faintly and from some place distant, notes from a wooden, edge-blown aerophone.

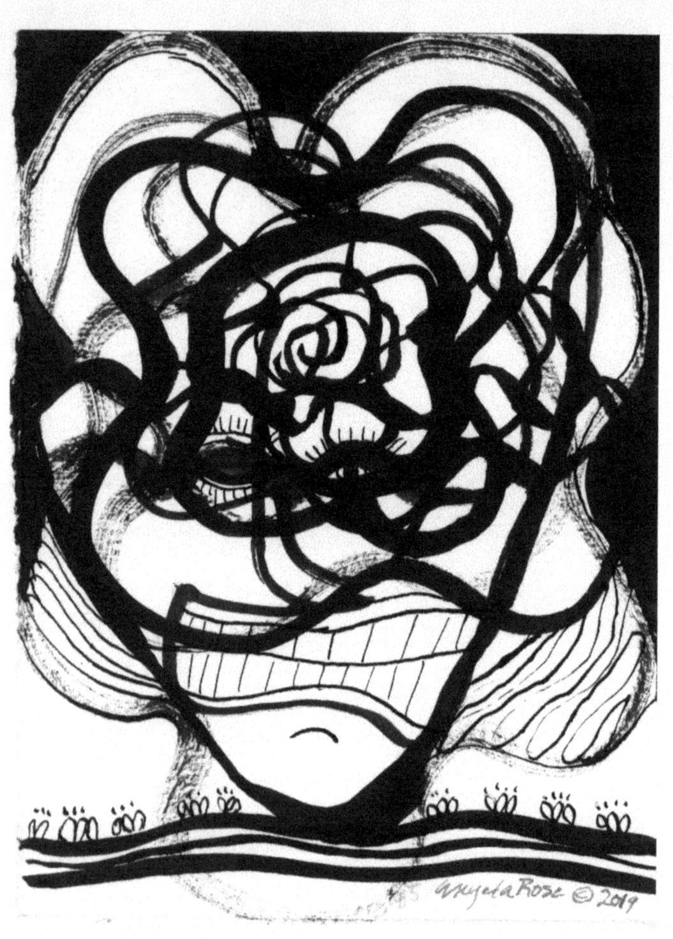

#5: Sometimes she listened to tapes of dark and convoluted messages.

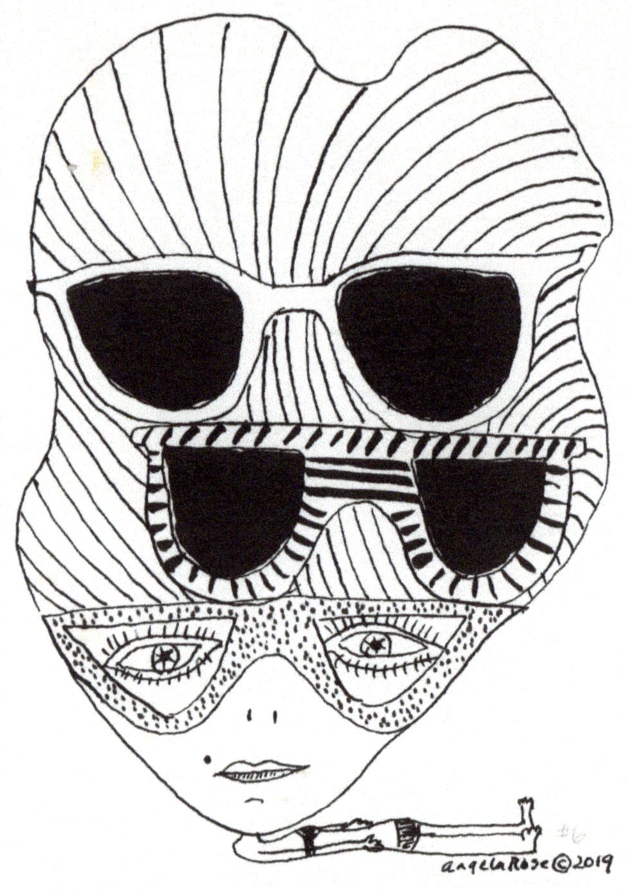

angela Rose © 2019

#6: Every other Tuesday she made herself small
and long and thin, like a tube of toothpaste or oil
paint, and squeezed with the full force of her
consciousness, thus releasing one large clear idea
at a time.

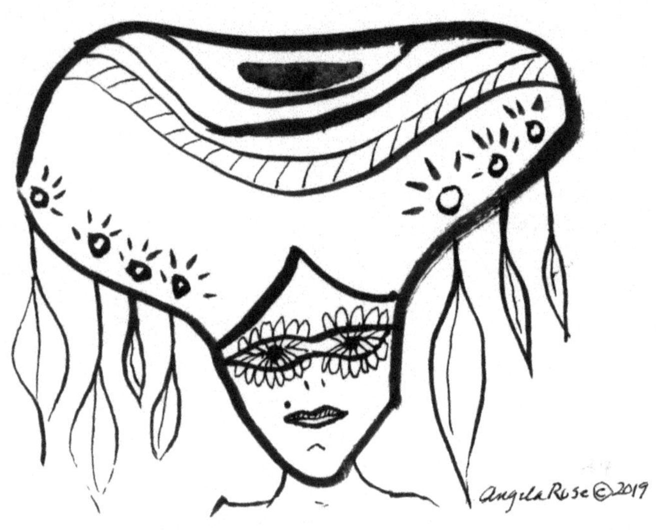

14

#7: Ideas popped like popcorn and she delighted in the expansion of her cranium, giving thanks also for versatile headwear.

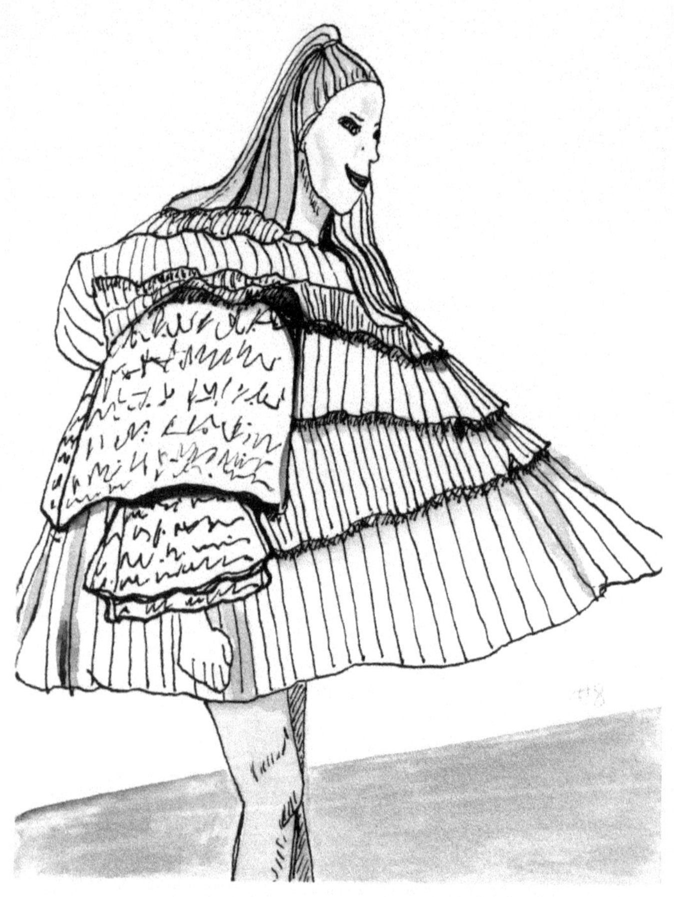

#8: She began to billow; streams of script sprang forth.

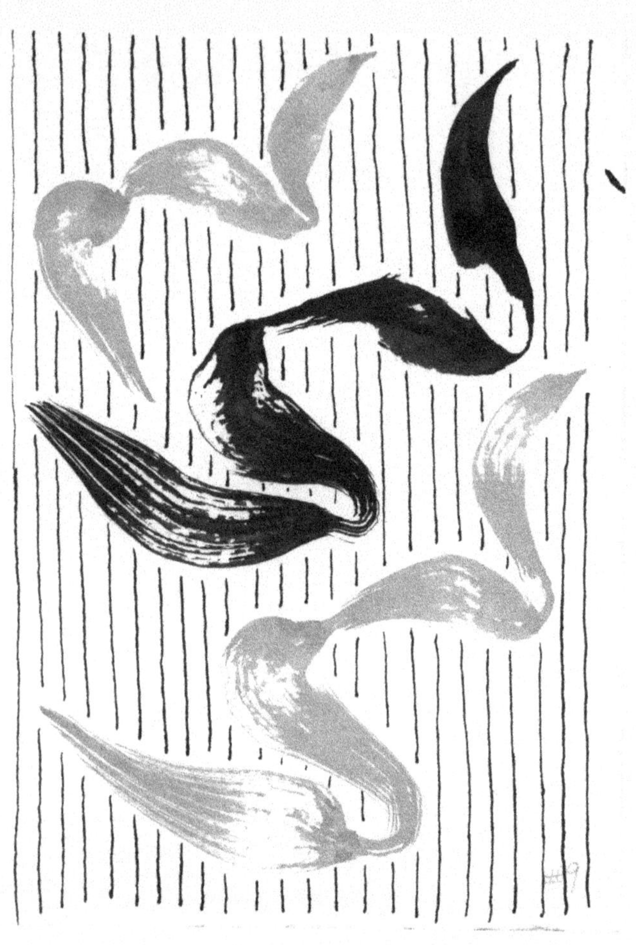

#9: Who hasn't hungered for that energy (call it erotic, call it the (in?) tangible tension felt in proximity to alive contrasts, call it a listening that happens in the body's every cell simultaneously)?

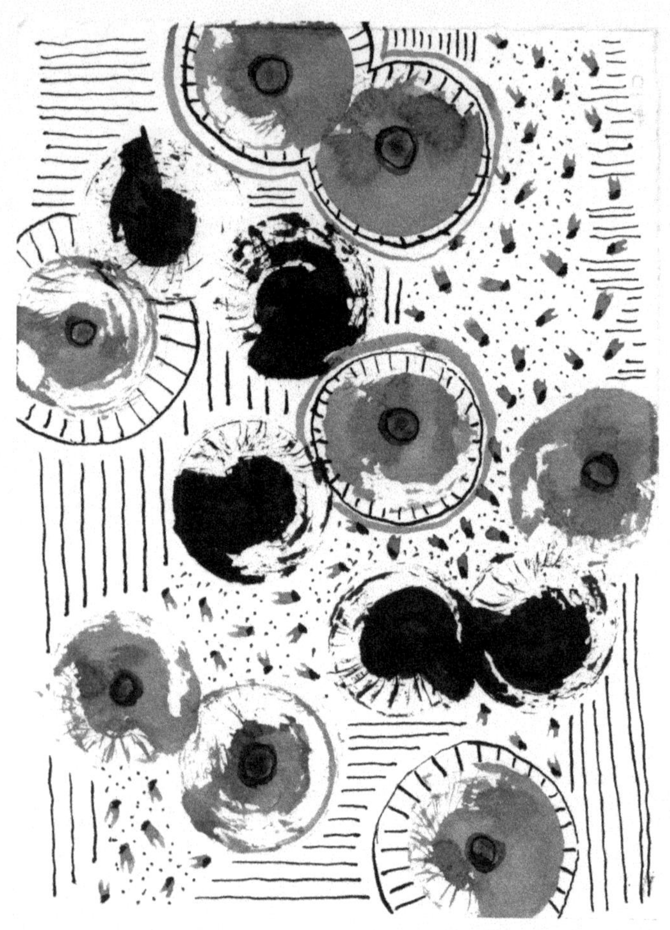

#10: Sometimes, she knew, to be most keenly alive meant appearing to all the world like a lump or heap, cultivating wouwei, while inside her, rooms and hallways everywhere opened, and invisible and minuscule beings began their journeys, passing through her towards destinations and creations to which she could contribute only by not interfering with their passage.

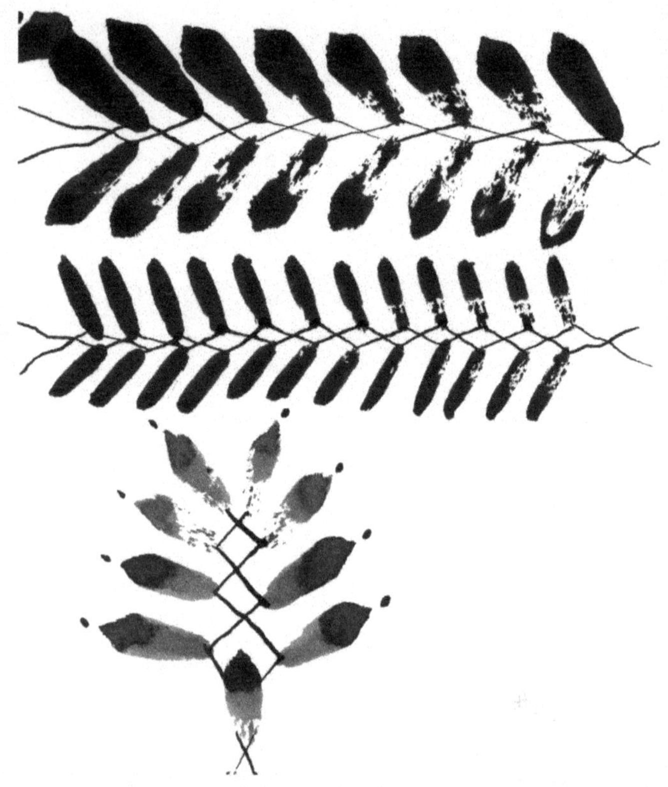

#11: Most of the insects, winged and un-winged,
go by unnoticed, not biting us, not asking advice
or stealing our shoes and hats, and we do not
bother with them, but then, sometimes, a
moment itself comes alive, and we are stopped in
our tracks and marvel at whatever passes our way.

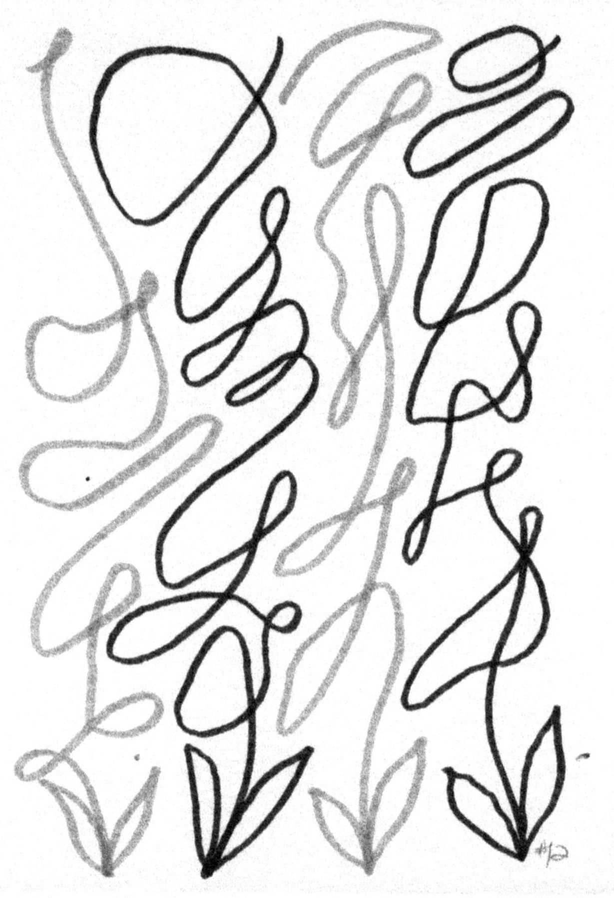

#12: Mornings, propped up against her pillows,
she liked to sit in bed, drink coffee, and watch as,
one after another, ideas began to flower.

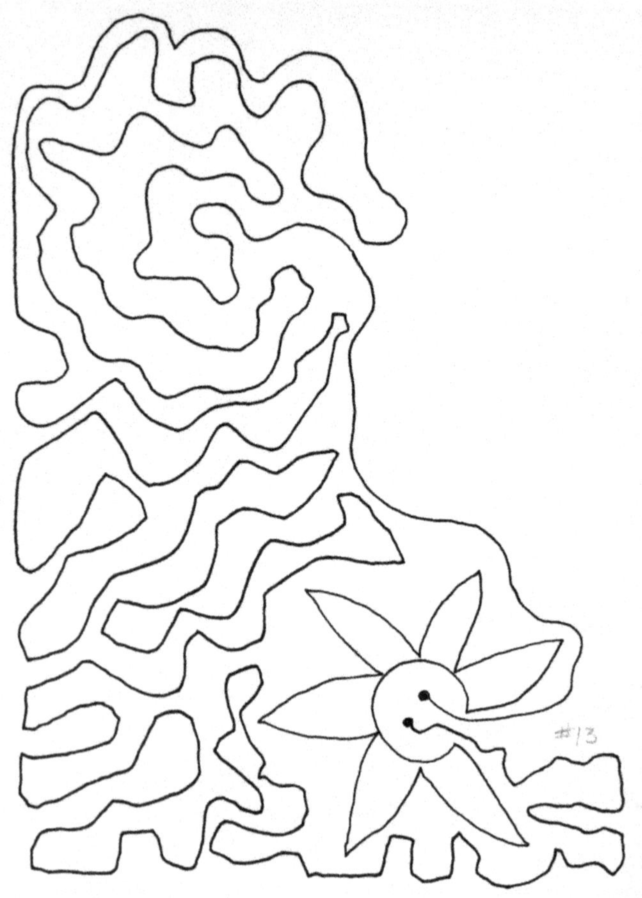
#13

#13: She began to conceive approximately 937 distinct shapes joy might take.

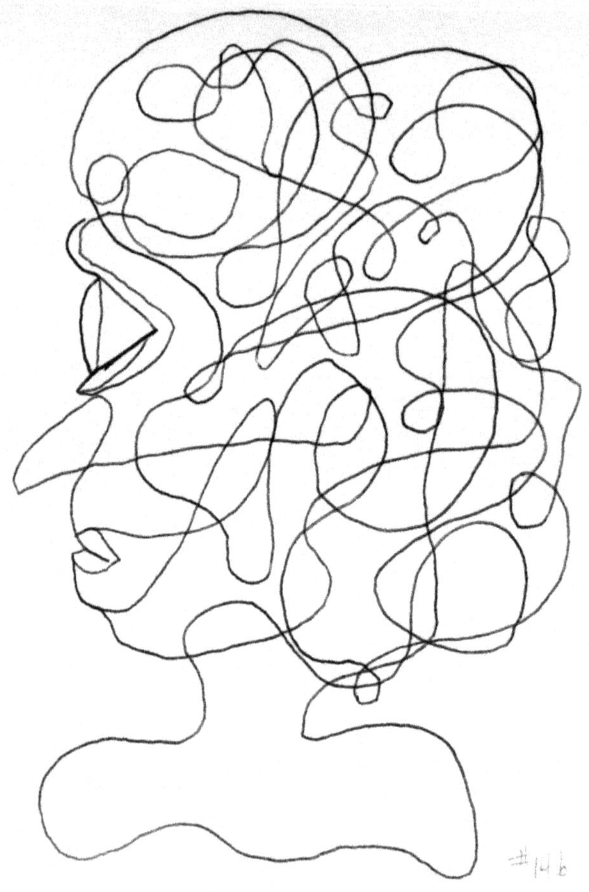

#14b

#14: Could a new hairstyle articulate the line of
thought that had brought her to this moment?

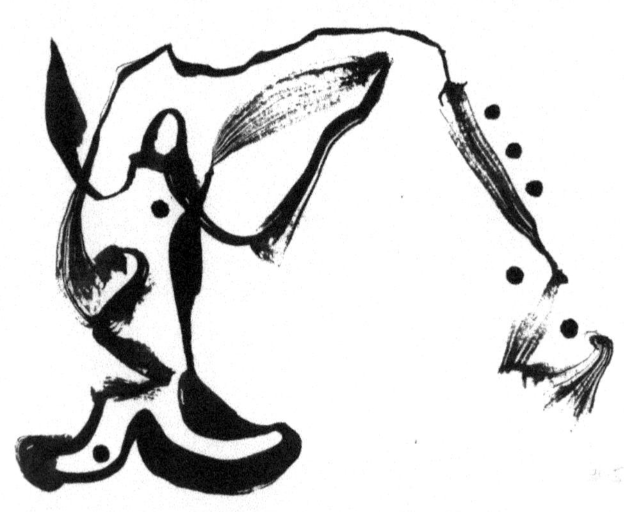

#15: She tossed ideas out one after another and watched them take shape, lying, falling, following, and still, she sensed, her best idea, the one she was most curious to meet, had taken up residence in her foot for now.

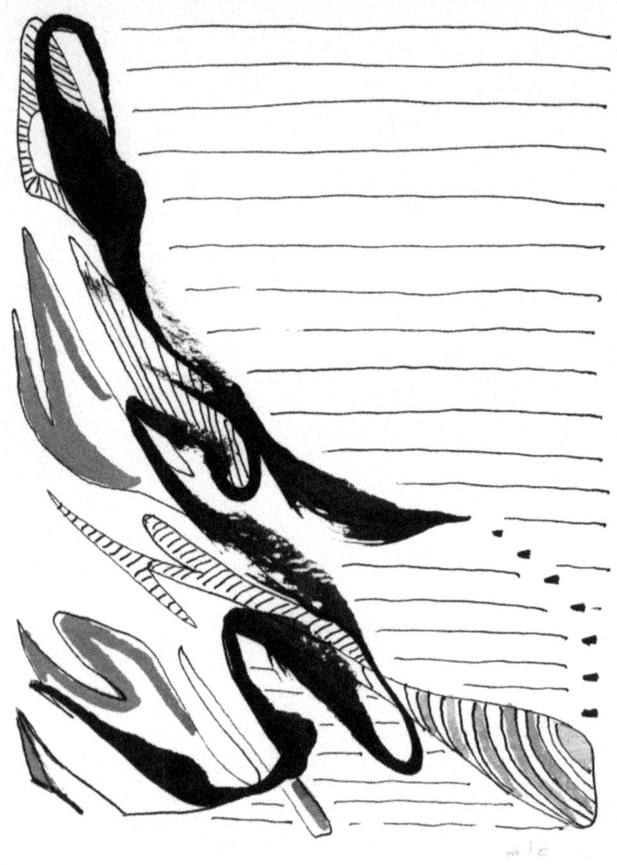

#16: She ran the fingertips of her deep
consciousness along the ridge of her own resistance.

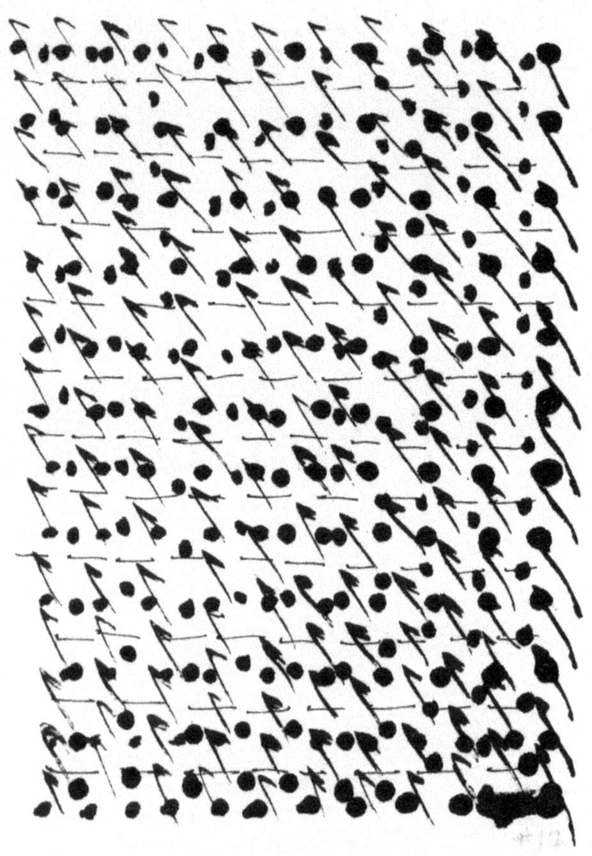

#17: In her purse, in her pocket, in her
shoulder socket, in her shoe, when she shivered,
in her liver, in her lung, on her tongue and her
lips, in her hips, in her hat, in her heart, she
carried one verb, one six-letter word—listen.

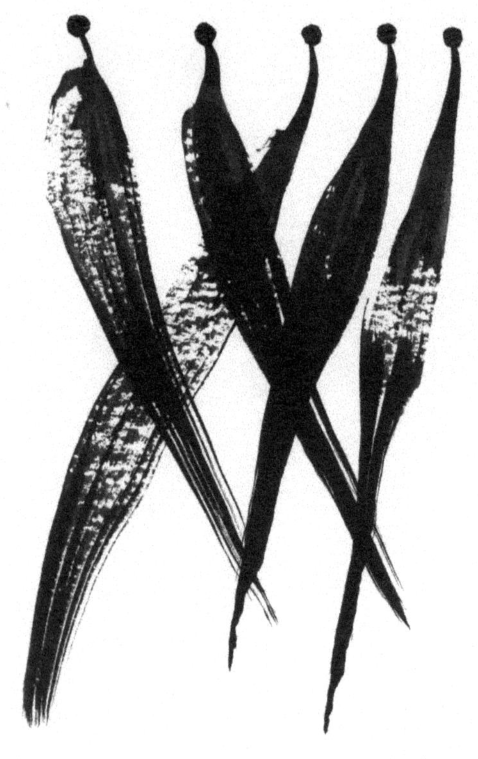

#18: Without even asking, she knew they must be the ones people called The Elegants.

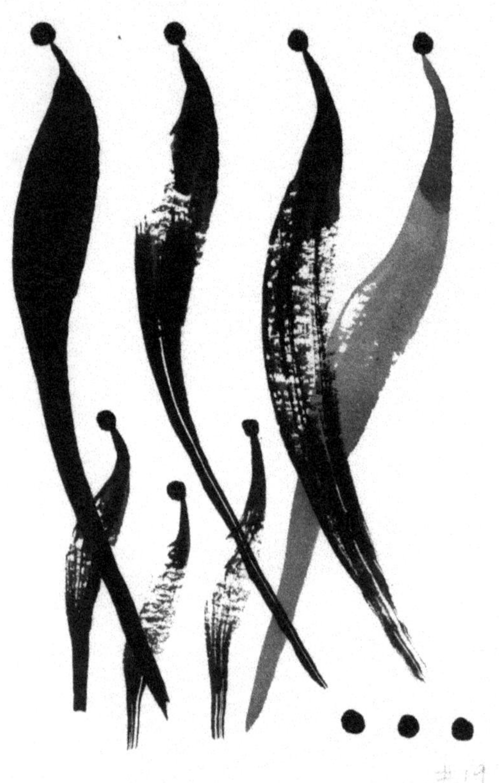

#19: And what would happen, she thought, if she remained so open that an entire parade of beings passed through her, each taking with it a touch of her rich darkness on its hat.

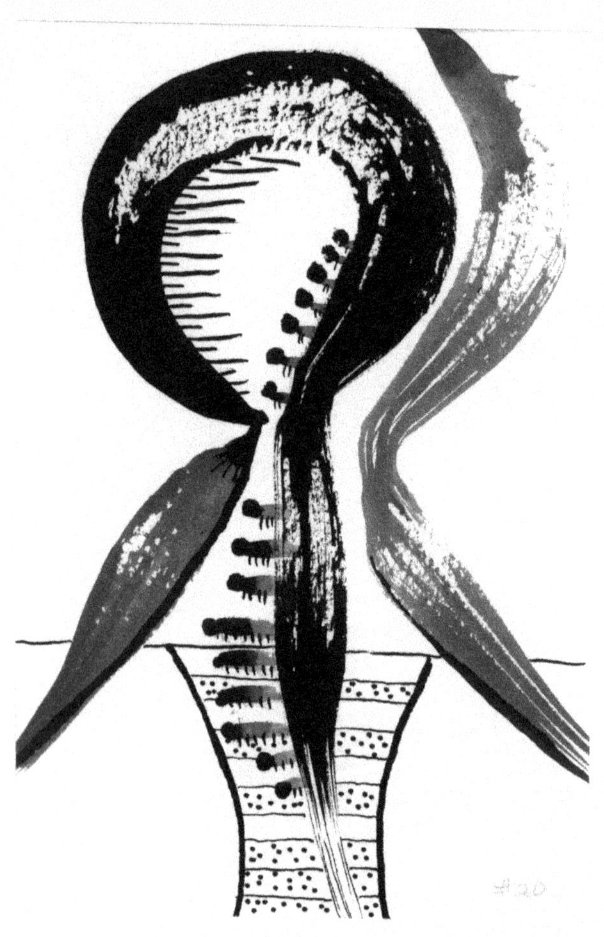

40

#20: She felt sometimes as though her skin was a
stretchy elastic sack, or a thick elastic material of
the kind certain boots are made from and that has
to stretch to fit over your foot and that, once
pulled all the way up, conforms perfectly to your
ankle and calf, and that this skin held in numerous
beings, that she had inside her, just now even, a
group of 5 or 6 ducks, mallards, each with its wet
webbed feet walking about and quacking, and as
she opened her mouth she watched as one after
another the ducks flew out, and she sensed that
when the ducks had gone, the stretchy sack of her
that had contained them would shrink since it had
less to hold, but instead, she found herself
expanding, as if the space once inhabited by the
ducks and now clear was an entity that could, once
empty, itself expand, space somehow making room
for more space, so that she sensed she might begin
to occupy more and more space, even as she
experienced herself as a passageway through which
numerous and varied beings came and went.

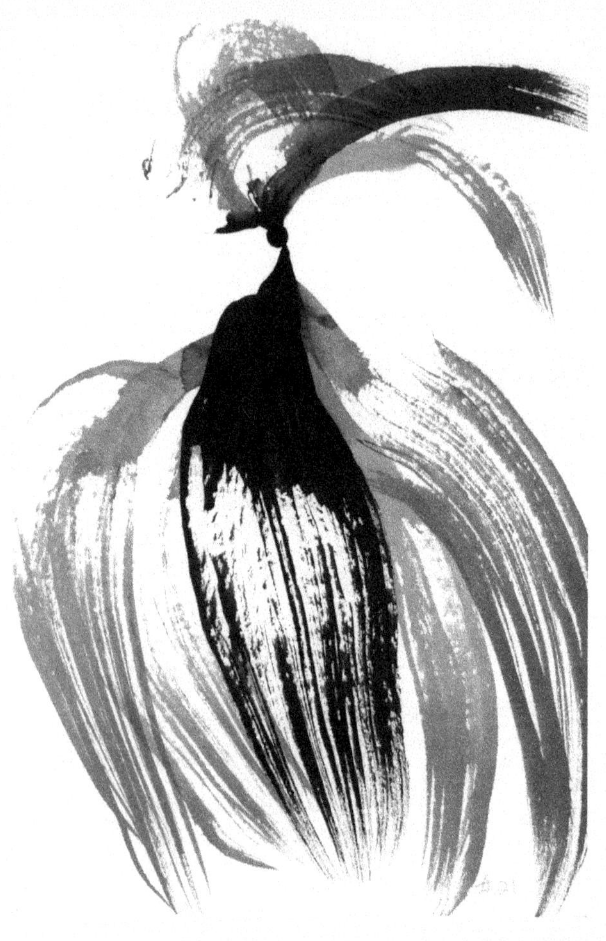

42

#21: Whirling weathers, windowed words,
wildebeests, womanists, wavelets, Wyomings—
wow and wow and further wow, she wondered,
was it possible that through so small a passage as
one small woman, oceanic energies might be
miraculously and continuously channeled?

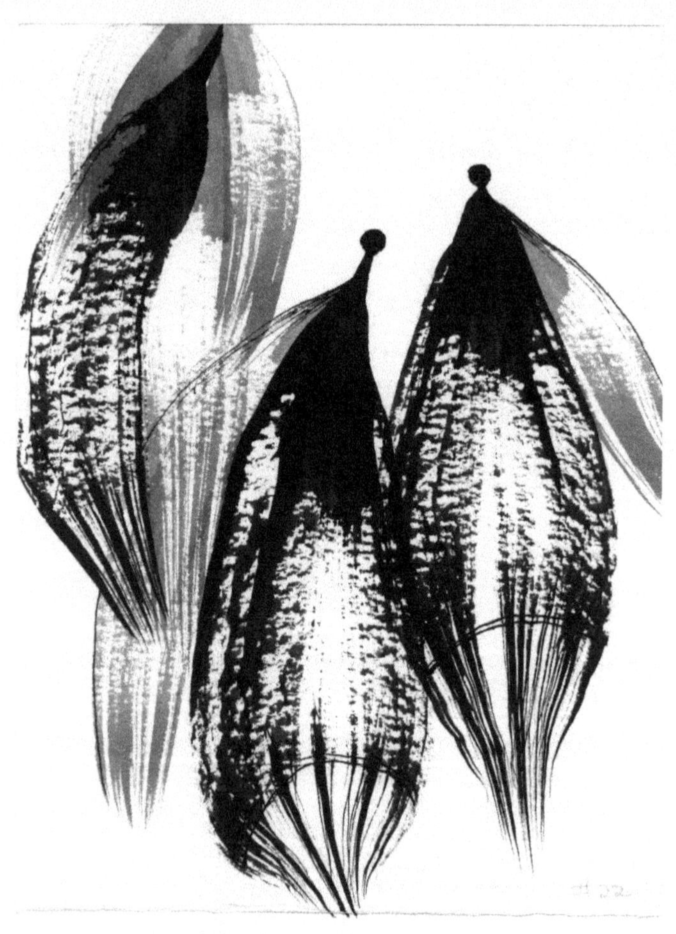

44

#22: She saw that she wasn't alone, not that she'd
assumed she had been, but she could see now,
clearly, that she was accompanied, that there
were other women with her on this journey, if
you could call them women, since each had so
changed they'd become like milkweed pods or
strange birds or enormous or minuscule angels
(scale had always been a matter that eluded her
definite perception), and one of these beings was
so close to her their energies brushed each other
as each marveled at her own transformation—
this opening, this filling, this expanding and now
this lifting off.

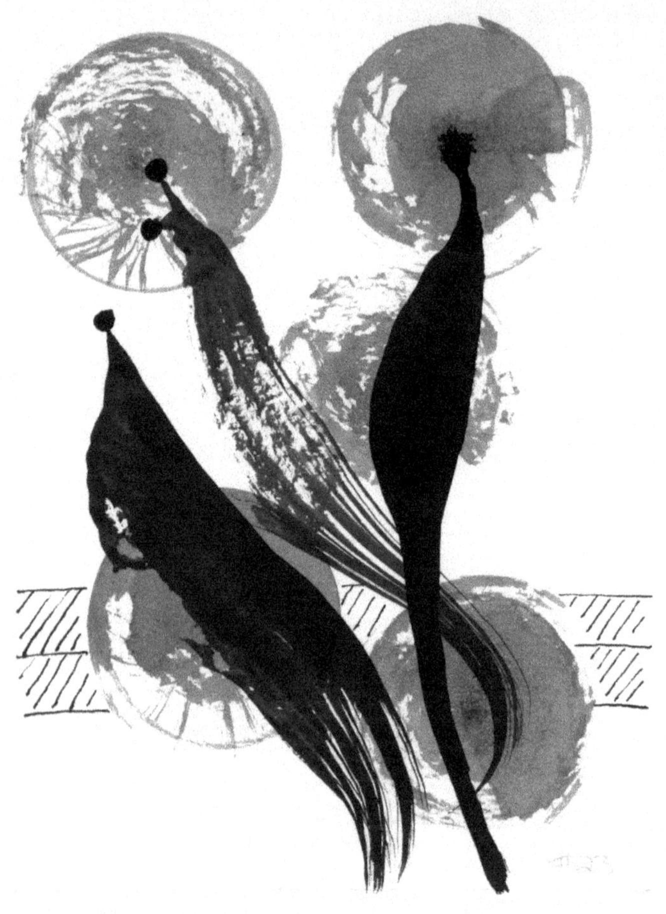

#23: They listened and breathed and gave birth to numerous worlds.

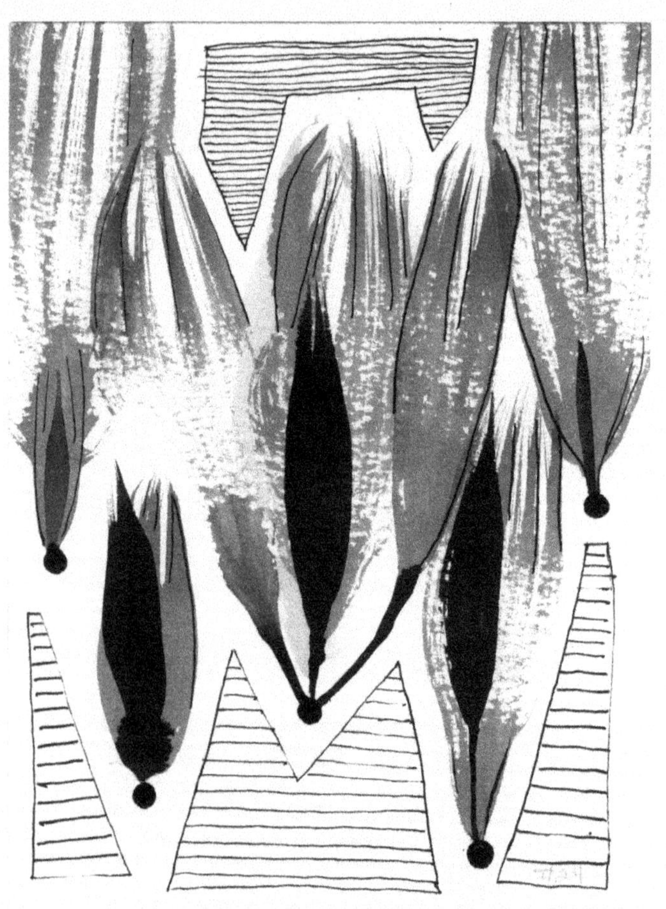

#24: And then it only made sense to enter the worlds they'd created, Eleanor and her companion traveler, and so one of them led the way though it was impossible to know who was leading and who following since they traveled through what seemed like psychic space as on a river current that shifted continuously and they, like leaves on the surface of that river, exchanged positions intermittently without any resistance until they found themselves outside the first of the worlds to which they'd given birth, a world that stood before them like some vast, glistening blue soap bubble it was possible to touch without its disintegrating, and they stepped through its outermost membrane and found themselves on a bridge from which they looked down into something—mirror or water or liquid silver—so vivid and still and reflective they could see what might have been their own images except they'd been multiplied, flipped on their heads, elongated, joined by others of their ilk, and in one image a division of cells seemed to be taking place.

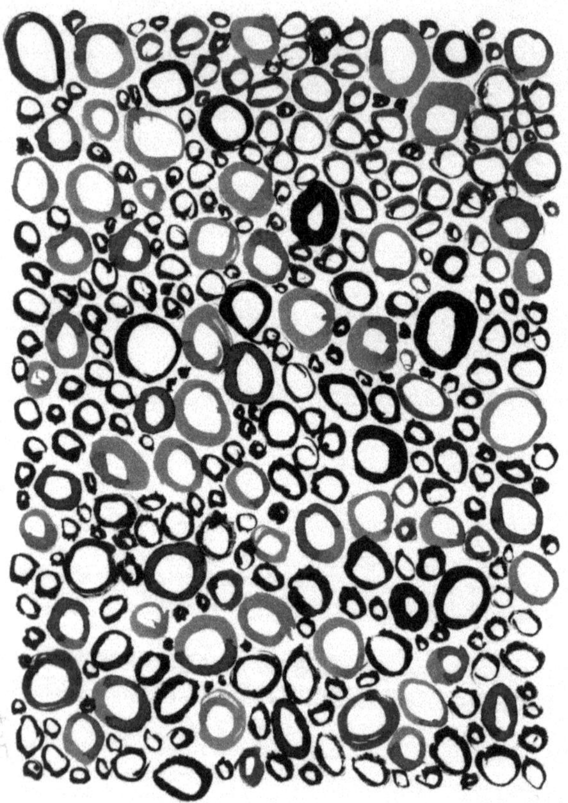

#25: It happens, she thought, that one can get lost
even in a narrative of one's own making, that one
can walk down a hallway in one's own home and
open a door to a room one didn't know existed,
that once inside, one may encounter women with
able though gnarled fingers and wizened
countenances, who stitch messages in red thread
into a cloak that, once finished, is intended to be
worn out into the world, a cloak that, though as
yet unfinished, has been awaiting one's
appearance for centuries, and though the room
may exude a degree of portent beyond one's
immediate apprehension, the messages might
involve instructions on how to carry with one at
all times a freshly uprooted carrot with which one
may point to the sky or a hawk, or which one may
employ as a prop while delivering a talk prompted
by a philosophical principle written in chalk on a
6 x 6 inch slate, or which one may swing about in
circles by its greenery while exclaiming the beauty
of Gertrude Stein.

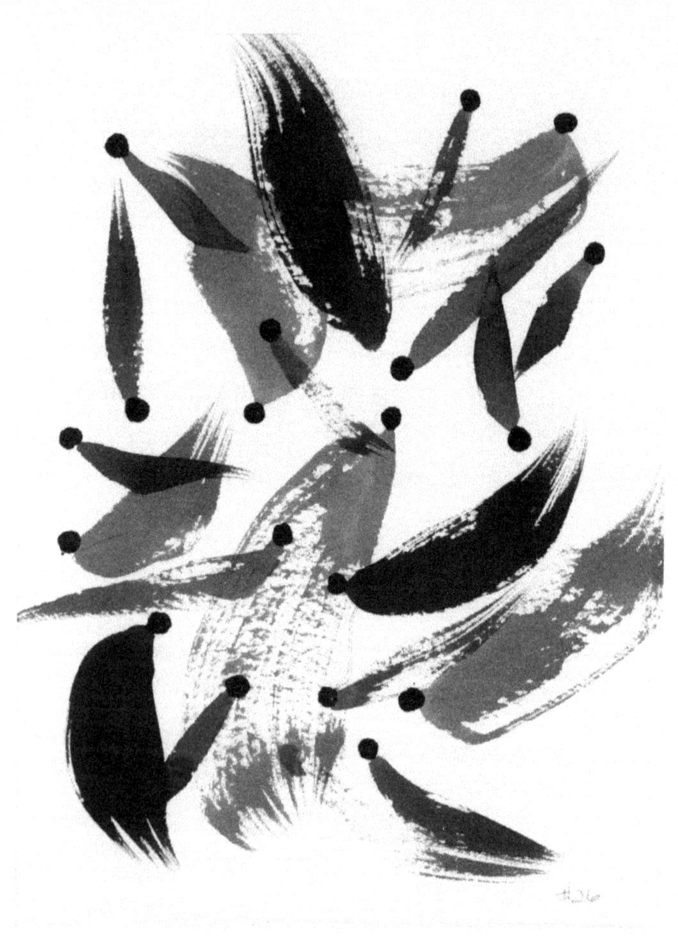

52

#26: There hadn't been anything remotely birdlike about her or any of these women, and yet, here they were, flying.

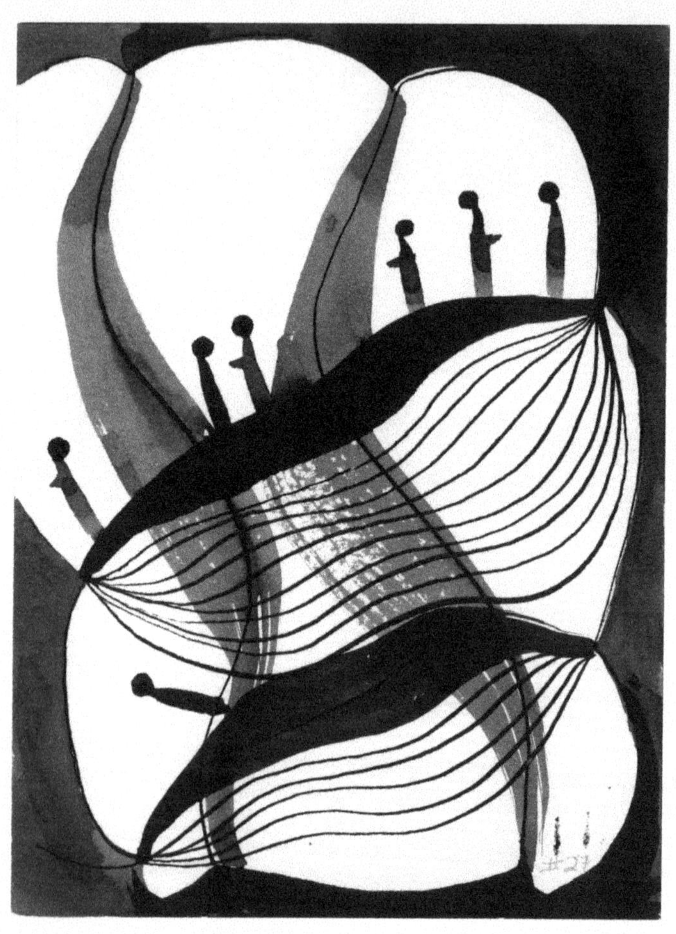

#27: And here they were again, examining from the inside the architecture of a single, tooth-sized seed of what would become a tree-sized idea.

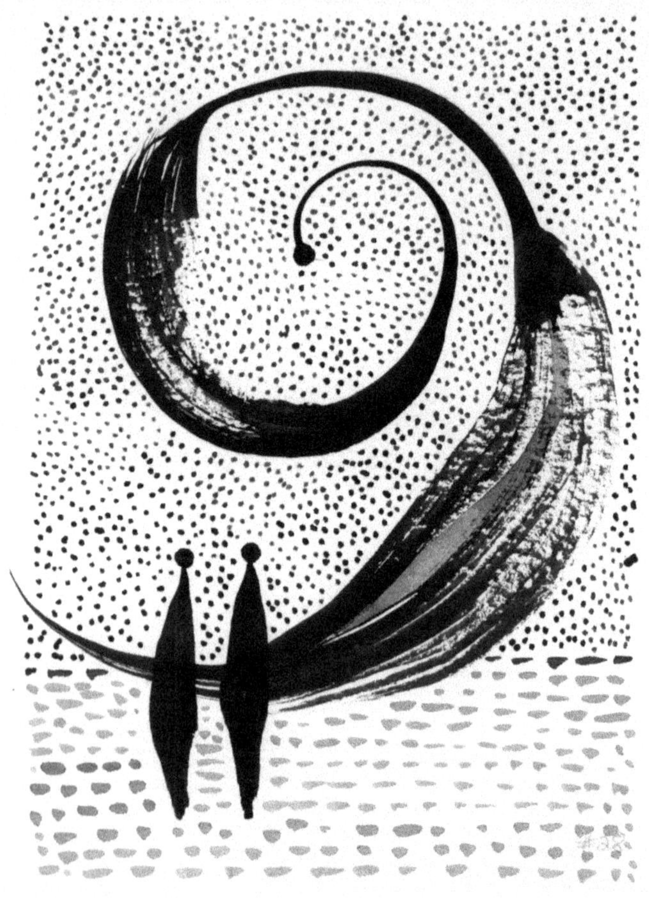

#28: "Sometimes," one said to the other, though
it was difficult for either to know which of them
was speaking, since they'd moved in and out of
each other's imaginative spaces so often and with
such fluidity, "when I glimpse inside one of your
ideas like that, it feels like we're conversing side
by side along a path moonlight's made on the
water, or we are about to slip in through an
opening of our own invention to board a spiral
that's all at once a seed pod and a chili pepper
and the crescent moon's distant sister."

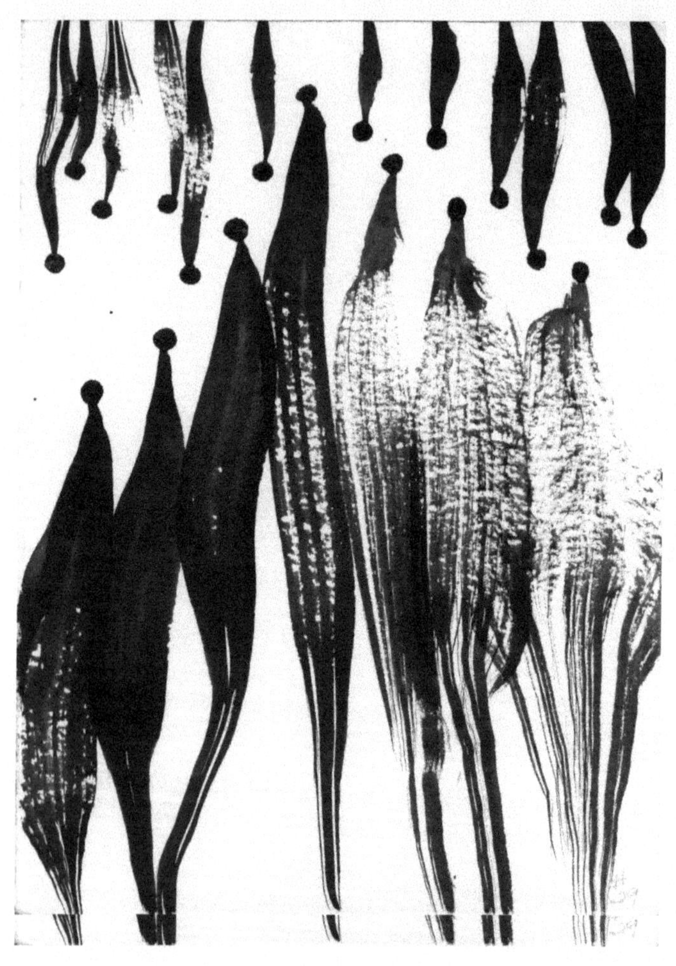

#29: There were throngs of people, rivers of people, currents of people all having one conversation, and while that conversation had several topics–she saw it like a braid in which the main strands stood out, their colors loud and drenched—what she felt drawn to, what she felt responsible for, what she walked miles and miles in order to open all the doors and windows within her for, what she learned to watch the figures who came and went through that house for, was another conversation, and all she could see of it right now was a fine strand of sky blue embroidery thread on which, barely visible, she could make out, as if with a magnifying glass, words and images that stitched themselves along, having no idea where they were going.

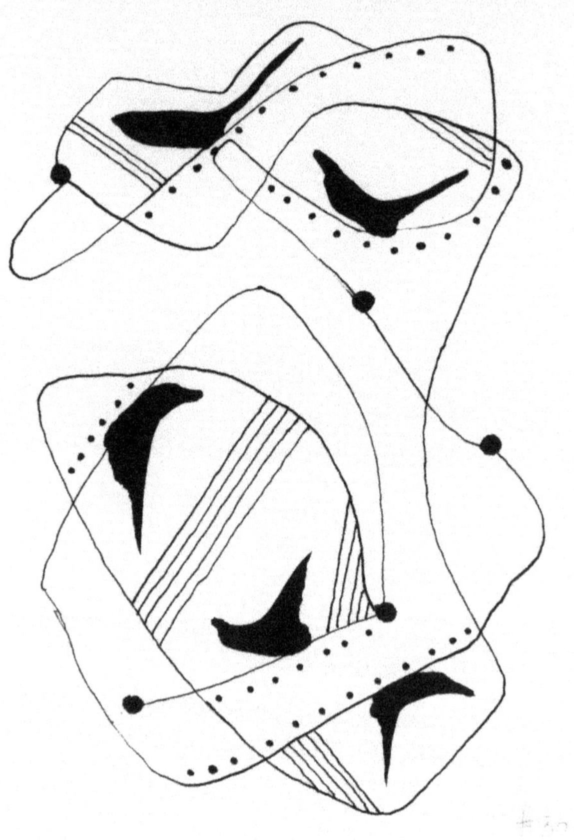

#30: She had heard people say a face is a map and
she'd never been entirely sure what they meant,
though she could read some of where a person
had been in their face so she supposed a face
could be said to map a person's history, which
might be useful in understanding how that person
came to his or her way of approaching colanders
and knives and dinner preparations and sleep, as
well as their understandings of love and art and
the satisfying use of an afternoon, but she also
thought she'd heard it said that a map was a face,
so she looked at this map spread flat on the desk
before her and located what she thought might be
a nose, and then another nose, and she began to
think that some maps were more than one face, in
which case she decided she may as well try to
locate the chakras on this map and follow the
most open energies, a method she imagined
would look like a cross between consulting a
Ouija board and memorizing the face of a
beloved with one's fingers.

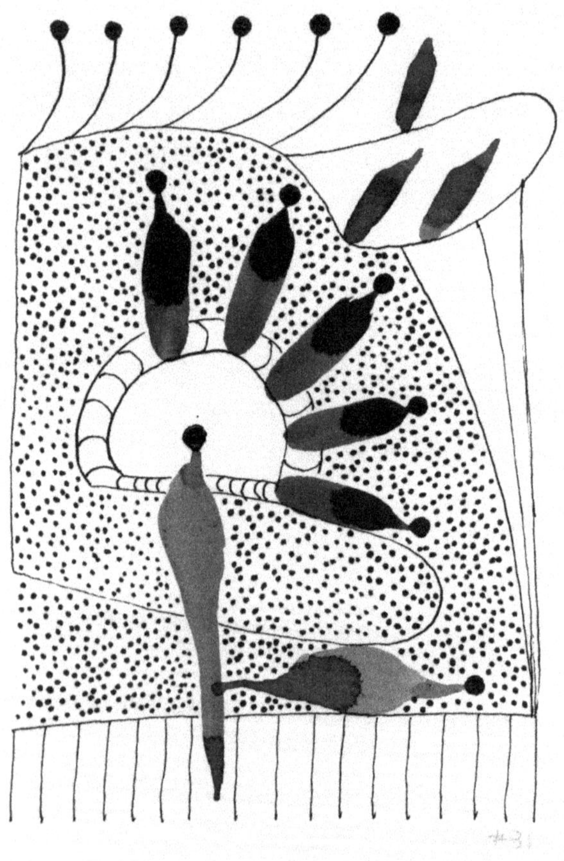

#31: She had often thought it would be useful to create maps of the places she'd encountered in visions, complete with stone-lined river beds, staircases that cut across dimensions, dining tables and small spoons filled with salt, and in the bottom, she'd sketch detailed legends that would offer scales for how time is measured in these vision worlds, as well as space and distance, and as she thought about these maps, she'd lie on her sofa, lay her hands one atop the other on her breastbone, tap three times and then begin imagining herself as a corpse, allowing herself to sink slowly and gently as far down into corpsedom as she could go, passing figures along the way who strolled in robes and head scarves and seemed to function as guideposts, and she'd smile to see that when she could descend no further, these figures would have just turned about and begun their silent ascent, leading her back to living.

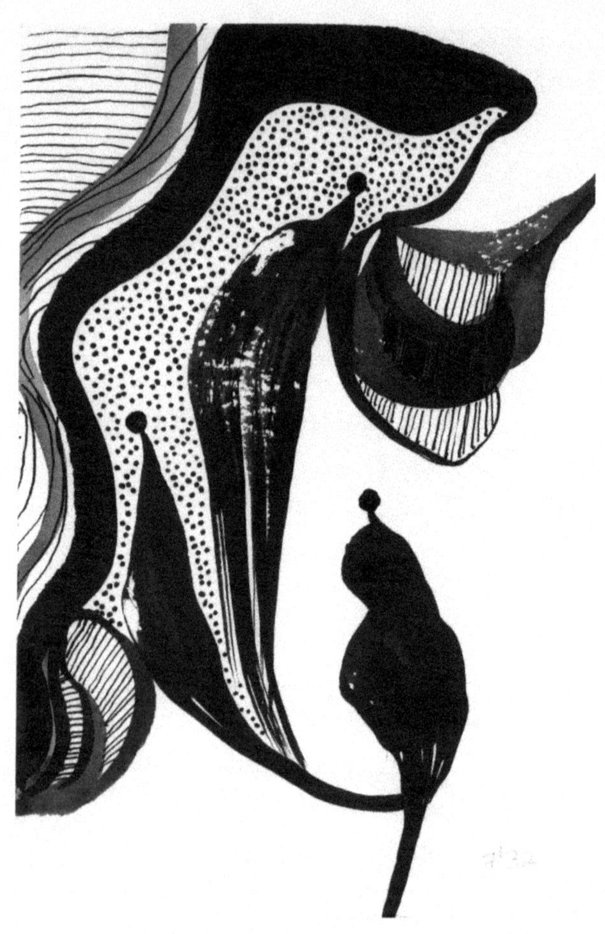

#32: Was she standing on a rocky crag, at the edge of an abyss, accompanied only by vultures and despair, or had she reached an opening to another consciousness, where gill-like creatures filtered souls and pebble-sized particles hummed with an unfamiliar, though beguilingly generative, energy?

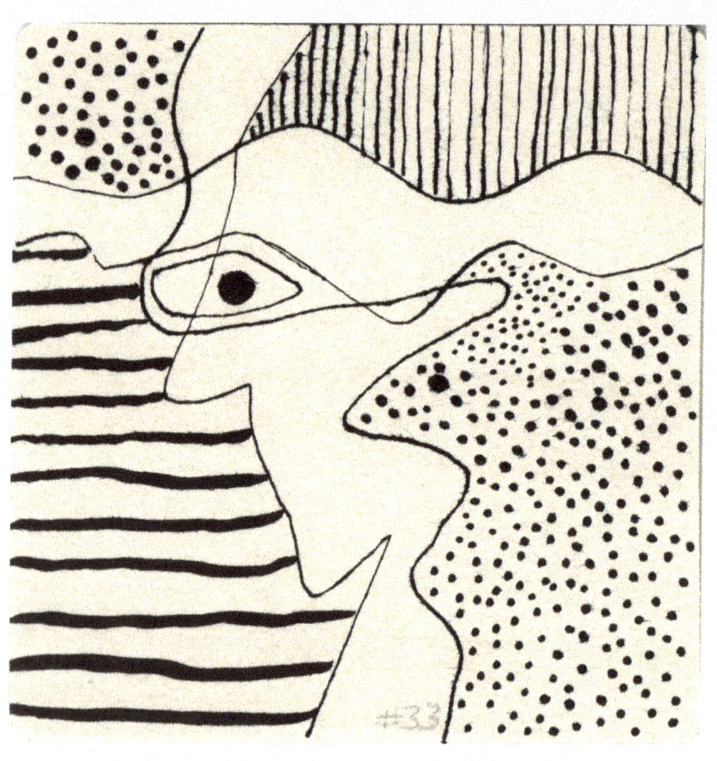

#33

#33: She decided to begin a new practice, a daily lying down, directly on the earth—on grass, on sand, on dead leaves, on pine needles, on pavement, maybe even puddles—allowing her cells time to accustom themselves, to begin to experience, one breeze at a time, one ant, one shiver, one worm, one stone, the inevitable reintegration into earth of the matter that is her.

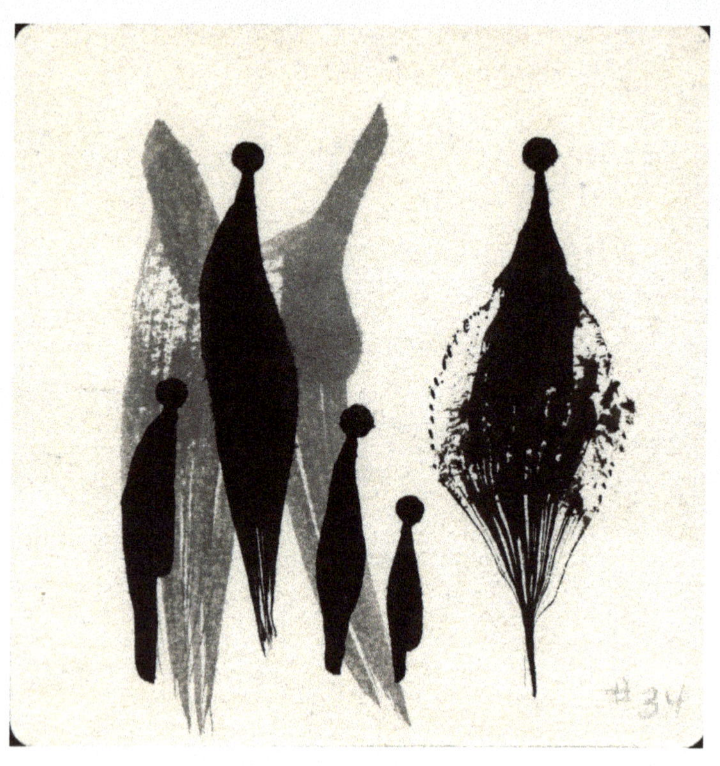

#34: Down at grass level, in the midst of a minor wave of fear, she began to acquaint herself with a new sense of scale and wingedness.

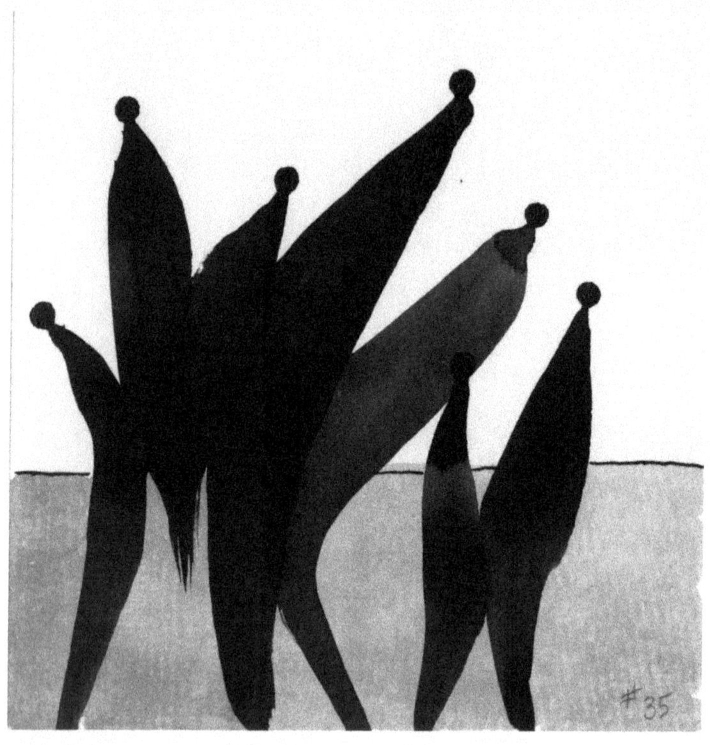

#35

#35: She asked, lying there with grass beneath her, little grassy points poking into her here and there, as she watched a white cloud move slowly across the blue blue sky and tried not to worry about disease-carrying mosquitoes and ticks, if she would grow more calm as she came to more deeply contemplate the connection between what lived and what is dead, since in the earth the two states so clearly flowed into each other that they might be considered segments on a single ribbon, everything living relying on things dying and already dead and decaying for the nutrients which then helped to promote and sustain life, and then, she thought, it's time to read "The Tibetan Book of the Dead," and she closed her eyes, and breathed, and then she saw small figures, antsized only standing upright and wearing small dark robes, gathering in the grass by her right ear, reading aloud to her about luminosity free from complexities, and she wondered what that meant.

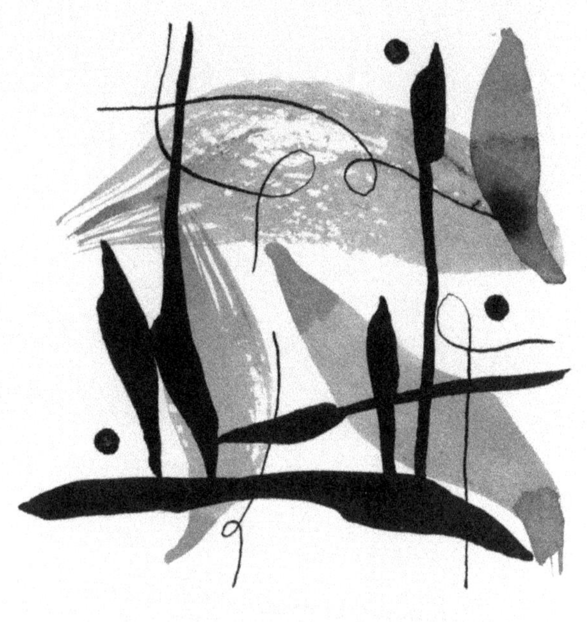

#36: And then it was as if she could hear the
earth tuning itself.

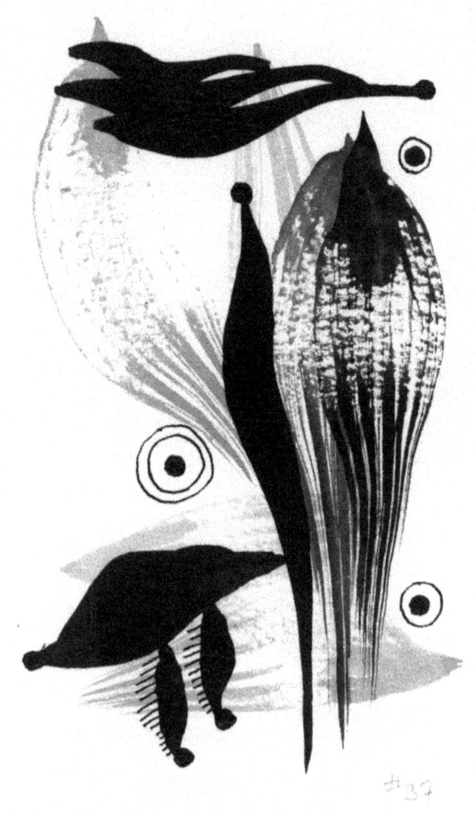

#37: Still lying on the grass, she continued to keep her eyes closed, listening, and she felt as if the more deeply she listened, the less solid she became, and the more she could not only hear but feel the hum of life and death beneath, above and all around her.

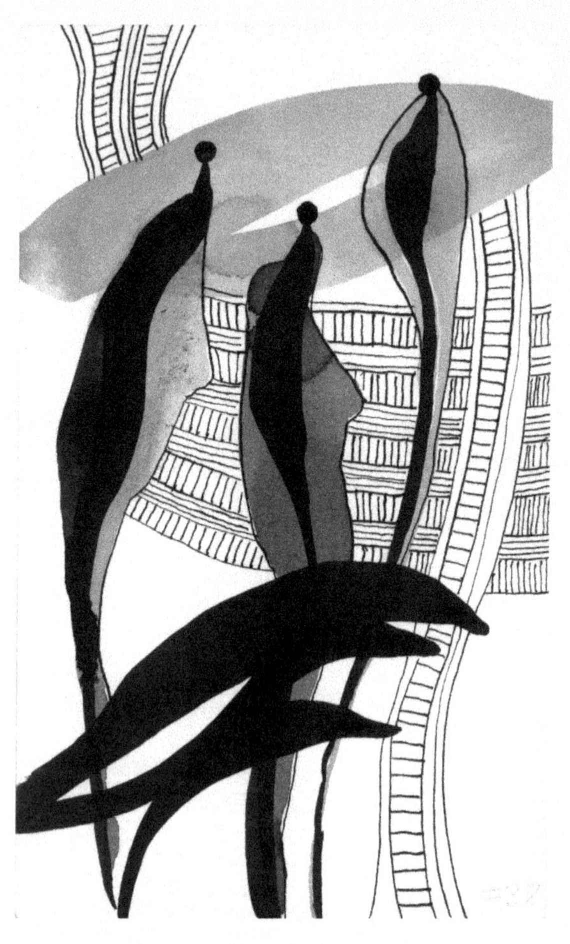

76

#38: And what if, she wondered, she could
continue in this direction, sinking more and more
deeply into the grass, traveling, by way of auditory
connection, into otherwise invisible stairways and
passages, rooms and gathering places, molecule-
sized cathedrals and lecture halls where wise
beings come and go, communicating in a
language of chemical transformations expressed
in song-like emanations untranslatable except by
certain moderately sized, lichen-covered stones,
humans who've been dead long enough to have
forgotten what a tongue is, and one or two living
artists who've learned to eliminate interference by
their own conscious awareness in their daily
artistic practice.

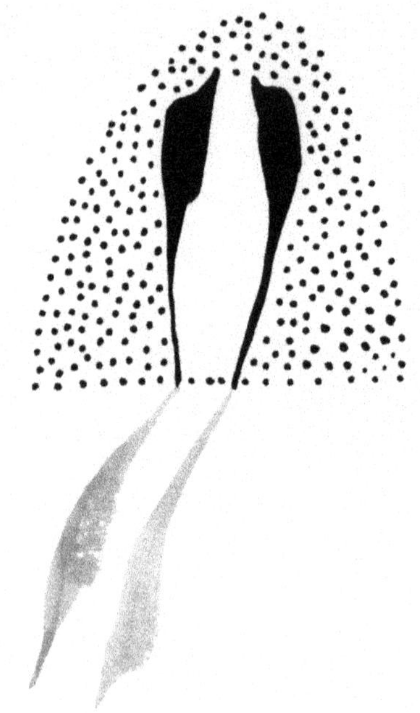

#39: Might she, might they, fellow travelers,
enter into a hive of being where there is always
room for the shadow self, a particled chapel that
composed itself especially for their arrival?

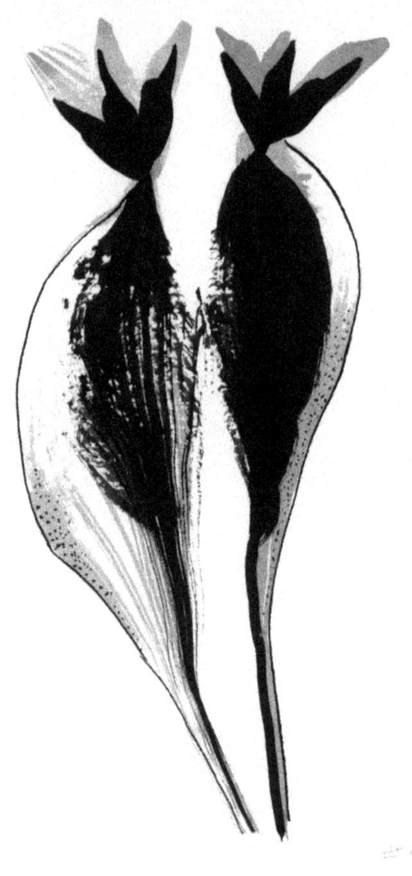

#40: Might they, in that space, unafraid of all
they have within them, allow themselves to open
in the caves, back alleys, and cluttered
basements, the primeval forests and deep oceans
of their unconscious, the tissues of their organs,
in their stomachs and lungs and intestines, their
bone marrow, in the farthest darkest countries of
their collective histories and dreams, and become
wonders, complex blossoming interrelated
structures whose language they discover they
speak fluently?

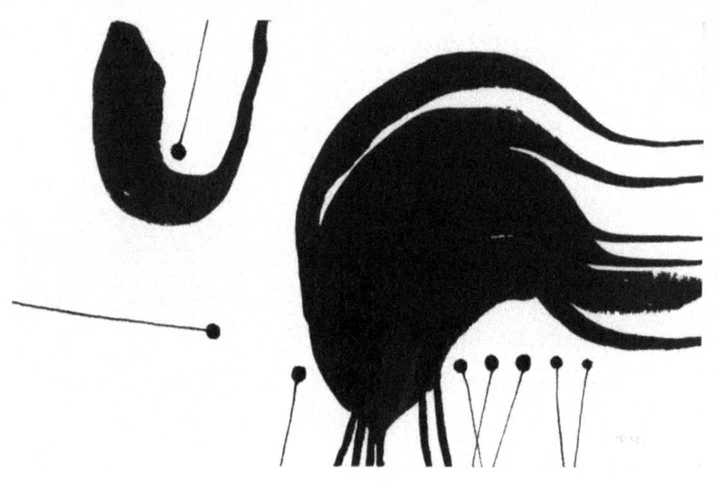

82

#41: They felt compelled to make detailed
recordings of what they saw—grasses, vaulted
buildings, unfamiliar hats, long thin shoes, etc.—
to do their best to translate what the voices they
encountered—were they the dead? or gods? or
beings from the ether or their own interiors?
—seemed urgent to express.

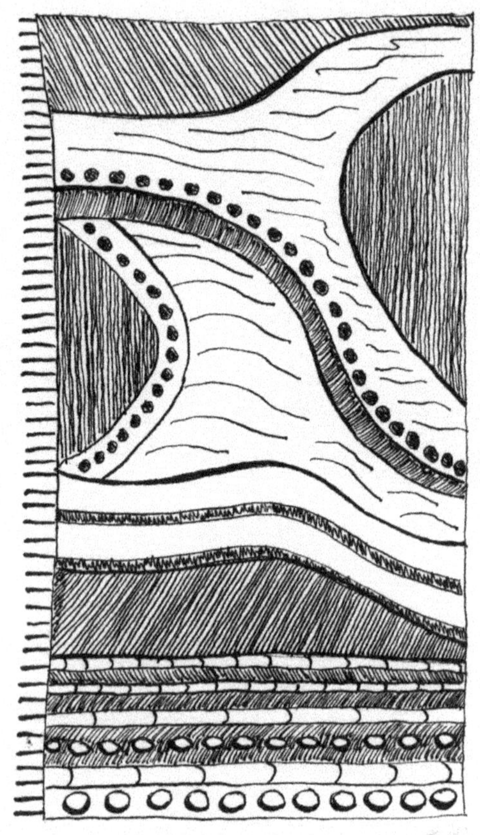

#42: According to "The Tibetan Book of the Dead," she recalled, there are very specific signs of near death and even more specific rituals for averting that death, one example being that if one notices the hair on the nape of the neck growing upwards (a sign of impending death), one must prepare a dough with black seeds, out of which one must build an effigy of the person one fears might die, one cubit in height, and into the heart of which one must insert crushed berries, the number of berries being the same as the age of the person, and after which one must make hair for the effigy from the person's own hair, smear its face with the person's own blood, wrap it in the person's clothing, paint it with black paint, walk it 21 paces from the person's dwelling, dig a triangular dark pit and toss it in, repeating 3 times, "Black demon! take this effigy!", then defecate upon it, cover it with earth and then go back and examine the person's neck; were these, she wondered, the kinds of messages they might need to record?

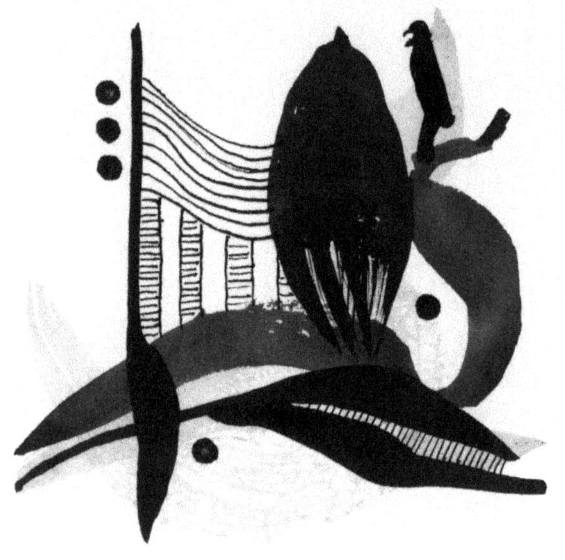

#43: One thing she knew for certain; they would
have to absorb into their imaginations the auspices
they encountered–the crow with its back turned,
the little female goldfinch dead on the path–and
allow each one its lyrical elaboration.

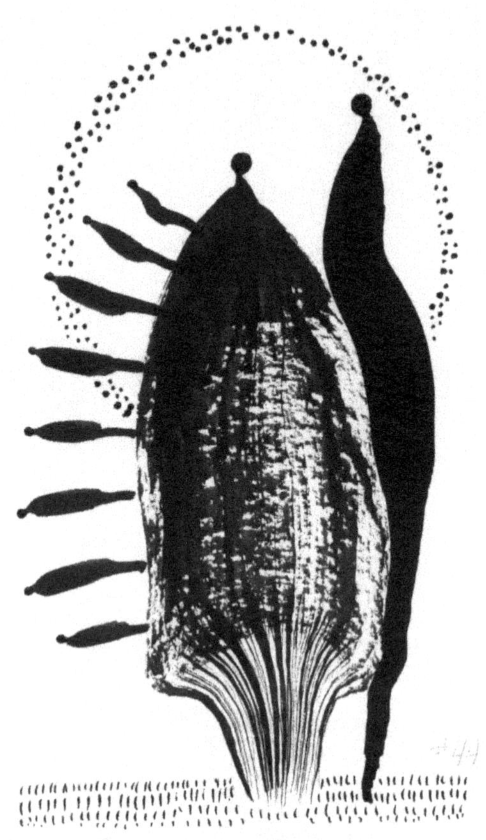

#44: And when she saw numerous beings walk
across the distance of her or her companion's
body—for each had become all at once
mountain, tree, horizon, lover, cascade, mother
ship, disciple, flower pod, light-field attached to
its own river-like emanation of ink-black
energy—she knew they'd need to hold all of it—
circle inside circle inside circle of subtly shifting
forces—as loosely as it is possible to hold any
magnificence.

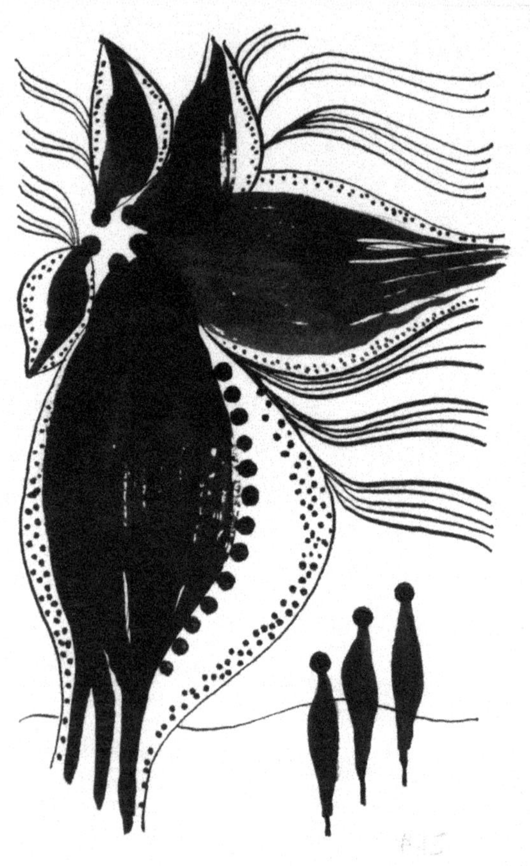

#45: They came upon several women who'd become one giant flower, their bodies petals whipping this way and that in a great wind, their heads, together as though in conversation, the seeds at the flower's center.

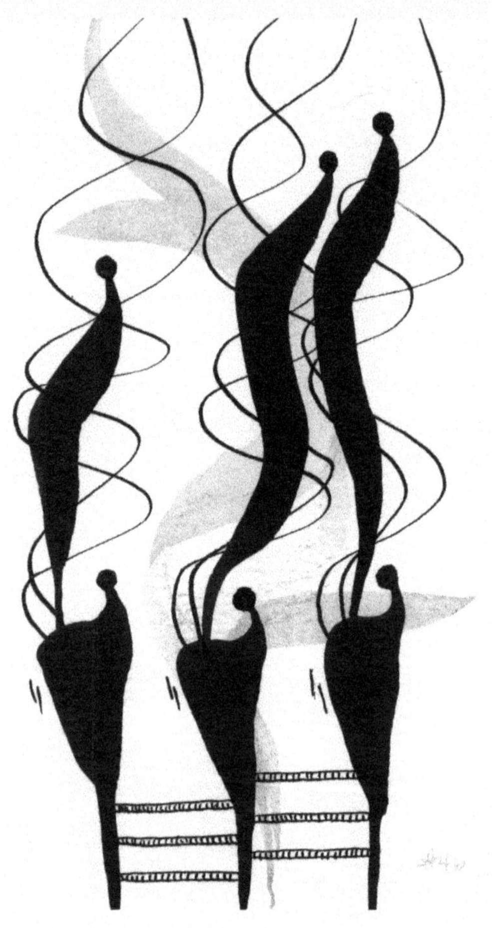

#46: Other women performed a meditative dance
on ladders, in the midst of which their spirits rose
out of their bodies like cobras or smoke.

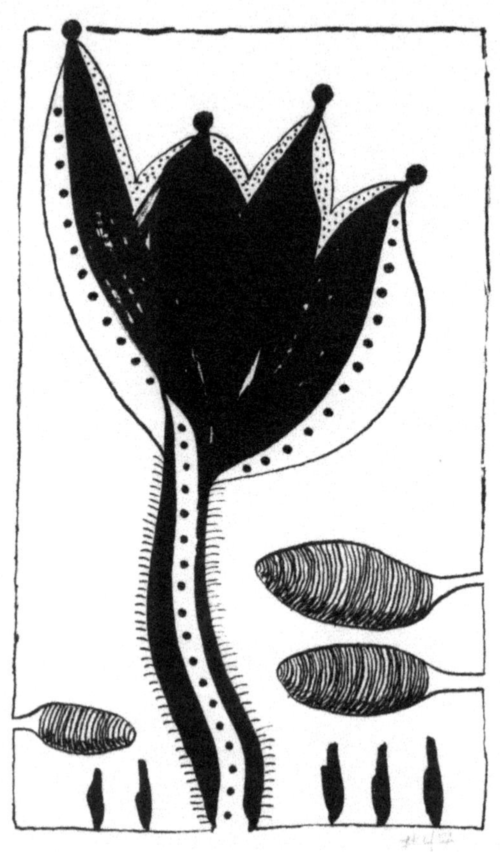

#47: There were women everywhere—some who'd become blades of grass among the other grasses, those who'd transformed into the petals of a giant flower and now rose high into a moonlit sky and looked out over a vast landscape, why even the stones on the road might once have been women, and all of them, if you listened with the fine hairs all over your body, were singing a song of regeneration.

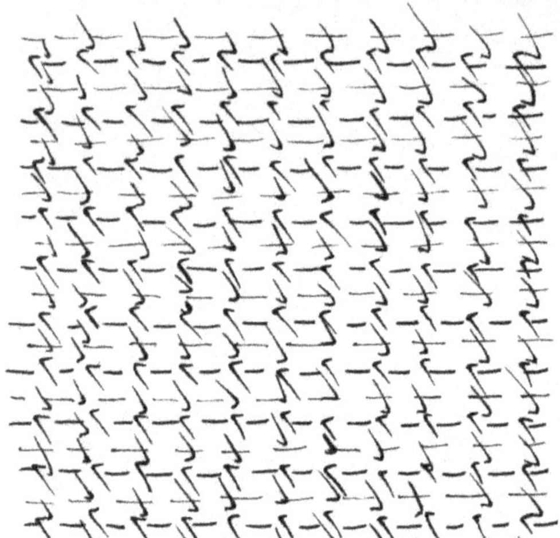

angela Rose © 2019

#48: If you ask her what she sees when she
closes her eyes, she will close her eyes, and it's
possible she will report a sandstorm, a musical
score, bird migration, men with scythes
harvesting wheat, the moments of her life flying
past, each one with equal emotional charge and
velocity, and now the camera zooming in and in
and further in, the notations on her heart from
every experience of love loss longing discovery
witness, samskaras from a lifetime, and further
in, another sky, deep space–how is it she hadn't
noticed this vastness before–and in this inner
cosmos, a whole new collection of constellations,
and what she senses might be radio communi-
cations from the dead.

#49: She began a new calendar, a little like a lunar calendar with its crescents and balls and lopsided balls of moon, only her calendar denoted the changing shapes the current of love takes as it courses through her like light, maybe most like moonlight, or like water in a stream or trickle or drop or river, each day's shape marked in a box on the calendar so that later one can look to see if there's a pattern, to see if its prominence or partial absence is cyclical or merely the result of her morning exercises in opening, channeling, and she understood that her measurements lack any specific calculations or accurate metric, and indeed she doesn't even know what the marks in each box indicate, obstacles or presence, if the days when love flows most freely are denoted by empty boxes, indicating the space for a steady stream, unimpeded, through the heart, or if an empty box indicates love's absence, those flat days when one is all surface, one's doors closed, and no travelers pass through.

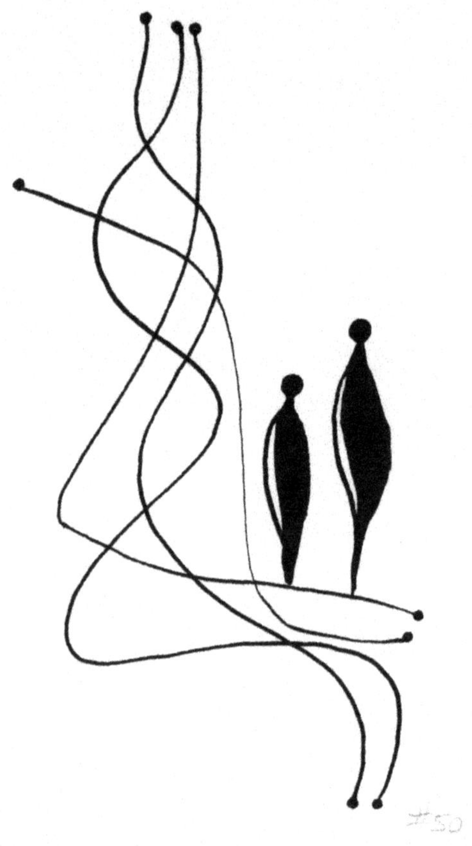

#50: Some days they found themselves standing on delicate, outermost threads of grief.

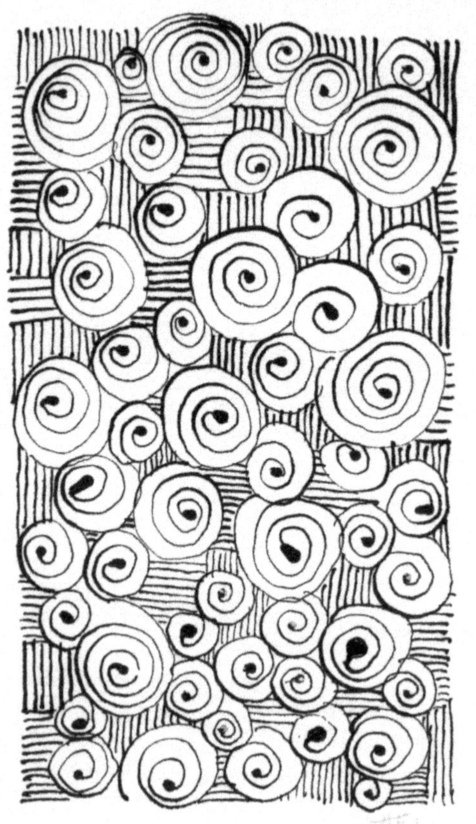

#51: She remembered how Gertrude Stein said there was nothing so exciting as diagramming sentences, and while she had to agree, she wondered what it would feel like to diagram plump rain drops falling on a pond, the intersection of two distinct imaginations engaged in collaboration, the impressions a mattress receives during a sleeper's dream of sitting under a quince tree watching squirrels scamper while the dream mother tends her hyacinths, or oboes conversing with violins.

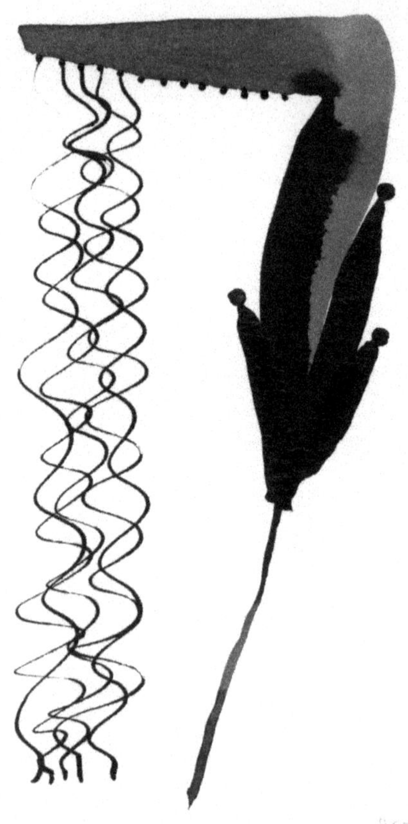

#52: They'd spent a good deal of time looking at the topsides of faces and flowers, books, organizations, shoes, ideas, favorite sweaters, paintings and sculptures and human relationships, and now decided to explore the undersides, the sources and their tendrils to other sources and shadows and the shadows of shadows.

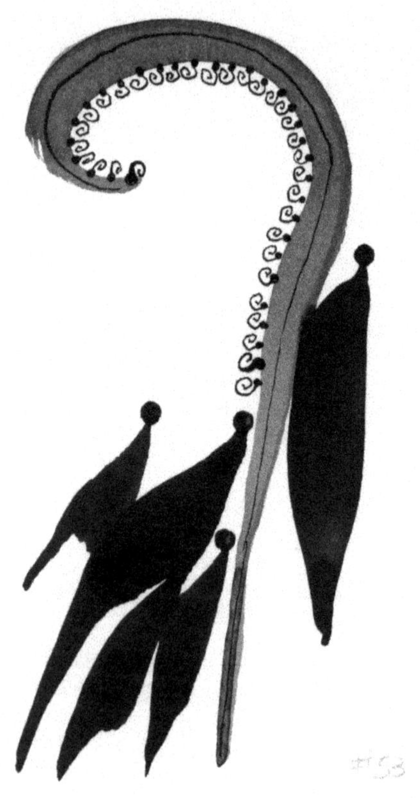

#53: For every shadow being they'd imagined encountering, there were 3 or more others they couldn't have anticipated.

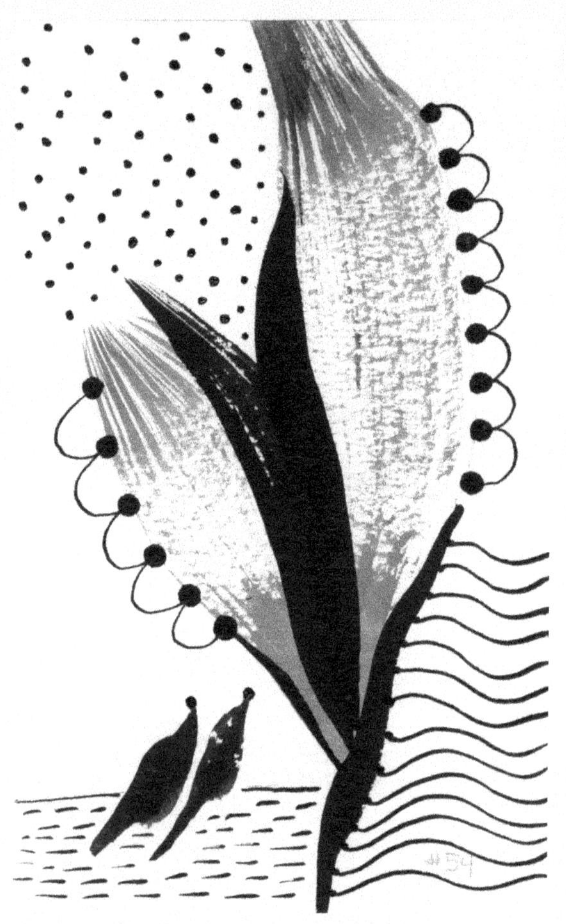

#54: It often happened that in the scent of a small cake dipped in a cup of tea, a man found his entire early life, with its two distinct walks around a country village, past hawthorn trees and a music teacher's living room window, past the house where, inside, his infirm aunt lay abed all day, past the church spire coming in and out of view, that he rediscovered his prolonged bedtimes listening to the rise and fall of adult conversation in the dark summer garden below and the bell announcing a late arrival; or that, in a crack in plaster or a secret compartment at the back of an old drawer, a woman found a hint of the lion or hawk or wolf who lived in her, awaiting awakening, with its power coiled in sleep, its appetite and musculature, its ferocity and keen eye; or that, willing to sit ever and ever more deeply into circles of increasing darkness, another woman found within herself the forests and fields, the alleyways and open boulevards, the pyramids, churches, passage tombs alit by sunrise on the darkest day of the year, and even the cosmoi, the ever widening, deepening darknesses punctuated in incomprehensible lights, awaiting articulation, awaiting lyrical elaboration.

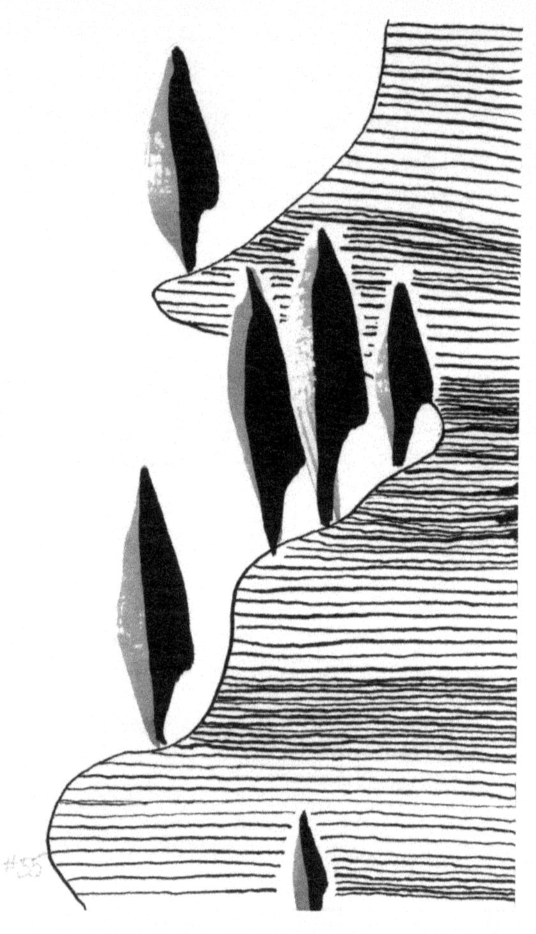

#55: There were moments when each of them felt it, as clear as fate—where to stand, which direction to face.

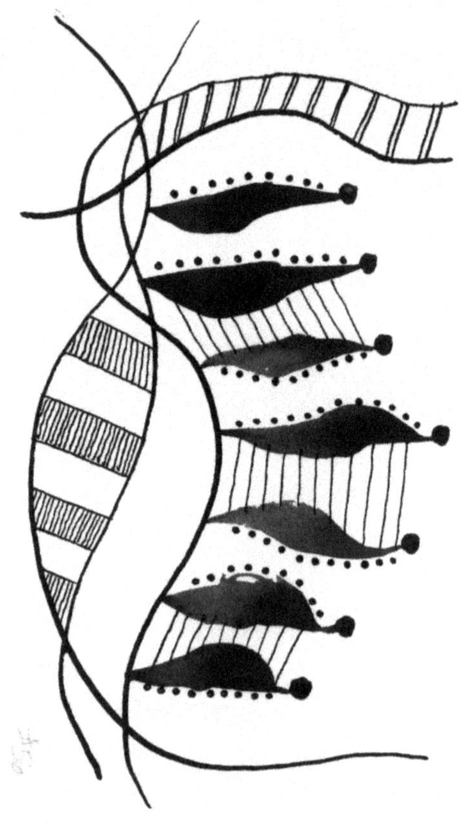

#56: One thing she liked about "The Tibetan
Book of the Dead," with its detailed instructions
concerning specific apertures through which
consciousness might leave the body at death,
each with its accompanying consequence in the
next life, was that it gave one concrete objects to
visualize and bring with one into intense
moments of being, such as one's own dying or
the dying of a loved one or practicing dying—
nostrils, for instance, and the value, which she
wondered at, of consciousness departing through
the left vs right nostril.

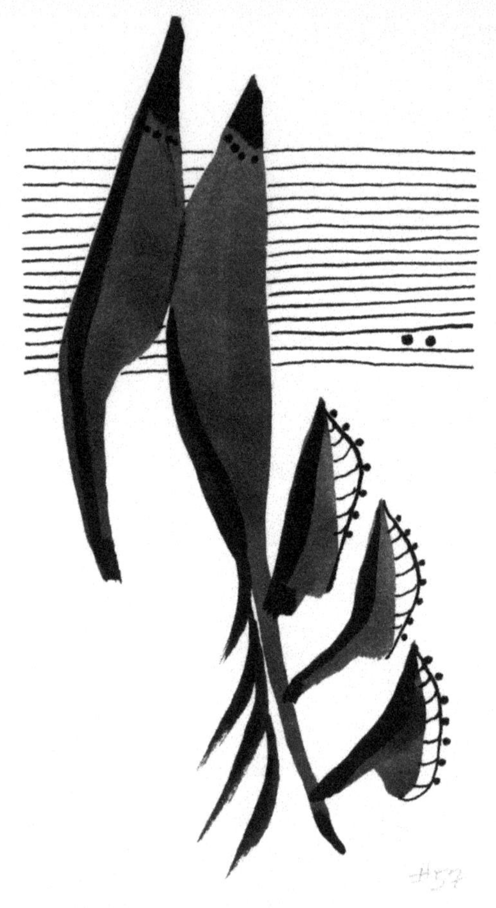

#57: There were days when a woman who lived inside Eleanor—call her her seated consciousness if you like, though often she wasn't seated but instead roamed from room to room and closed all the blinds or swept a floor or sat in the kitchen where she constructed shadow boxes that expressed knowledge she came to in visions—remained utterly still, and through a crack in a window blind, her eyes watched Eleanor's encounters with human society in such a way that Eleanor felt as if she herself had just arrived in the midst of a culture utterly strange to her, where humans collected to celebrate and declare and express possession and joy, to eat and drink and smile, and they gave her things, little slips of glossy paper with words and pictures on them, some tied with ribbons, and they sang songs, and Eleanor felt the strangeness grow from the size of a loaf of bread to a living room sofa to an entire locomotive until the strangeness felt so strange she understood only that she didn't understand the humans at all.

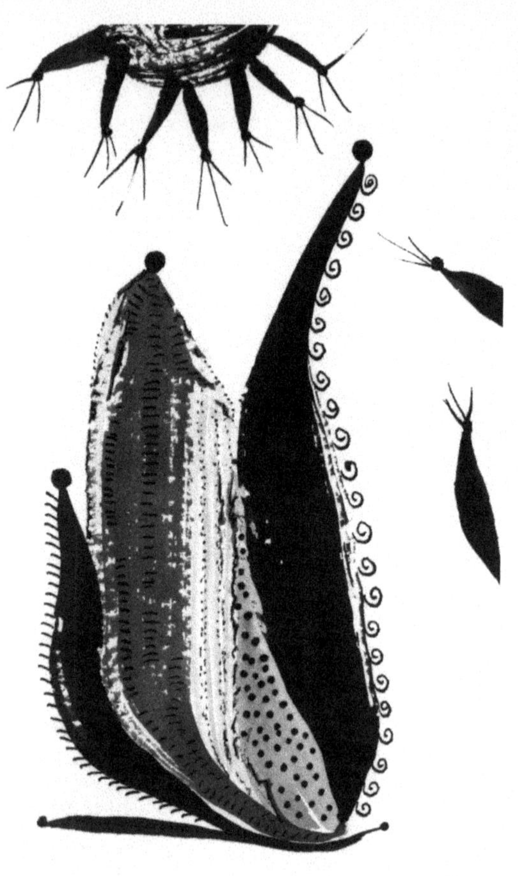

116

#58: When she looked inside, she laughed to see
the strangeness of the world multiplied right
there in the cabinet she called her self.

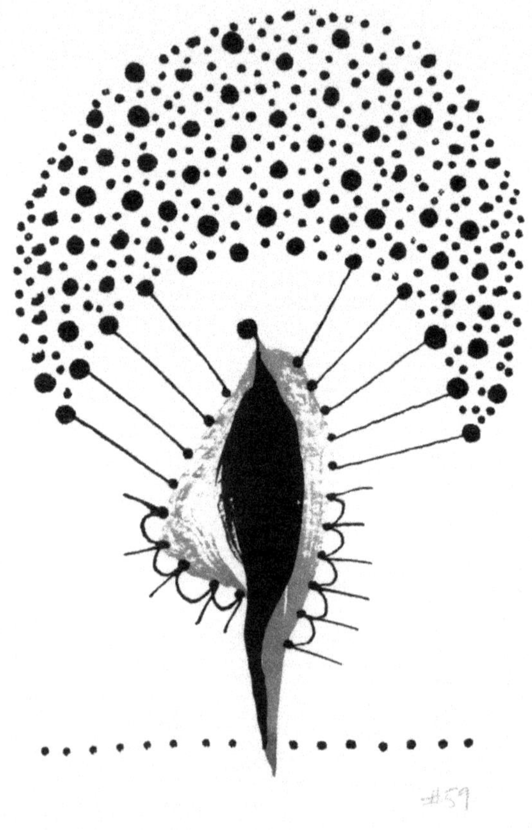
#59

#59: It had been a brisk and breezy Tuesday when she became suddenly aware that she could no longer tell the difference between emanation and reception, aura and parachute, radiance and puncture.

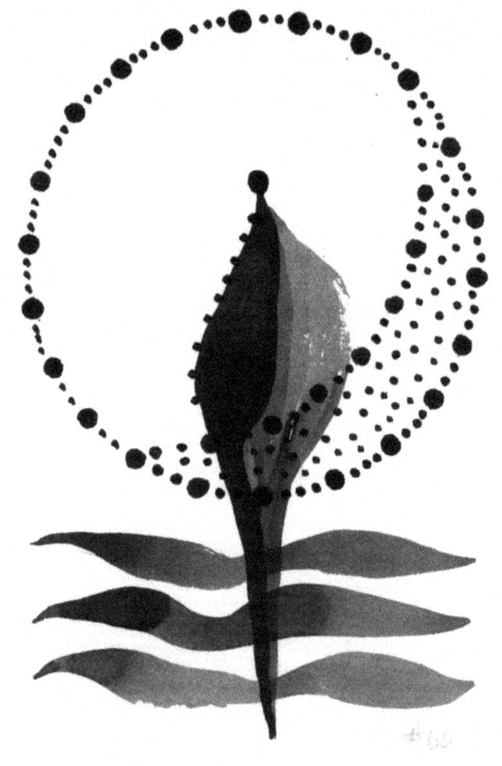

#60: There were moments, most of which
involved some combination of 1) either late
night or pre-dawn dark, 2) being alone, and 3) a
few ordinary objects such as a bedside lamp,
pillows, a book, a coffee cup and a pen, or her car
in the driveway, a lunch sack, keys, and
paperwork in a carryall, when she closed her
eyes, or opened them and looked up to see a half
moon on its descent in the western sky, and she
felt so vividly—radiance, emptiness, and
awareness—3 rivers, inseparable and
spontaneously present, running through her, and
all she had to do was be.

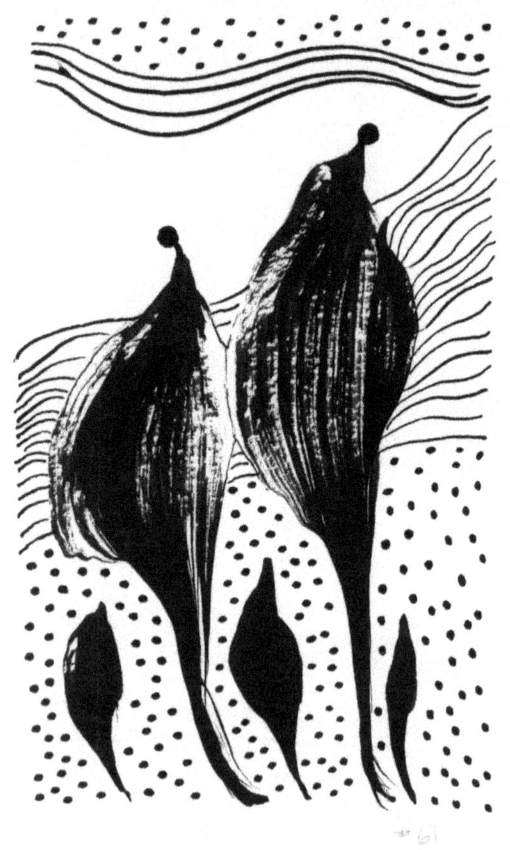

#61: "Whan that April, with his shoures soote /
the droghte of March hath perced to the roote /
and bathed every veyne in swich licuor," she said
inside her head, and then she said again, why am
I reciting Chaucer, unless I've been triggered by
the winds, which, oh Zephirus, can change
everything, including one's view on whether or
not one's life is like a jacket with big sturdy
pockets into which one has stuffed a book, a
handkerchief and a few coins, or if one has been
instead merely tossed hither and yon like a
namby-pamby bit of puff.

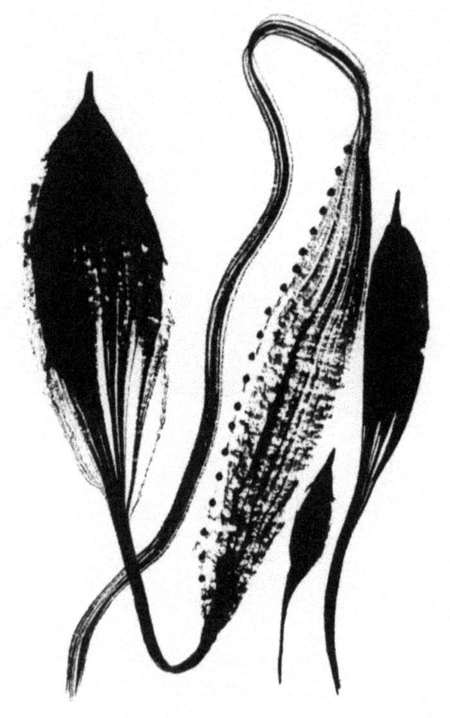

#62

#62: Sometimes it was difficult for her to stop thinking
about how the sun makes up 99.9 percent of the mass
of our solar system, which is pretty staggering when
you consider that the other .1 percent is comprised of
planets, clouds, rain, oceans, rivers, canyons, almost 8
billion humans and all their hair, skin, livers, noses,
lungs, maybe 700,000 African elephants, 1,000 species
of tardigrades (sometimes called water bears or moss
piglets, which have been around for 600 million years
and can live in dirt, water, leaf litter, patches of moss,
and possess the ability of cryptobiosis, meaning a state
of suspended animation in which they can go on living
even as they look dead), fields of sunflowers, marigolds,
butterfly weed, butterfly bushes, cows, cowbirds, ante-
lopes, orangutans, more than 356 species of turtles,
plus cardigan sweaters, lobster pots, ink blots, psycho-
logical testing manuals, automatic drip coffee makers
that burn coffee, bakers' hats, welcome mats, glass
display cases containing pies, bear claws, cinnamon
buns, breads, and scones, and then museums with
collections of bones of extinct mammoths and dino-
saurs, so much mass all rolled into one tiny tenth of a
percent inside of which, where do all the songs fit, the
arias and play performances, the memories, griefs,
dreams, the attractions, the ecstasies, the milkweed
pods, the migrations?

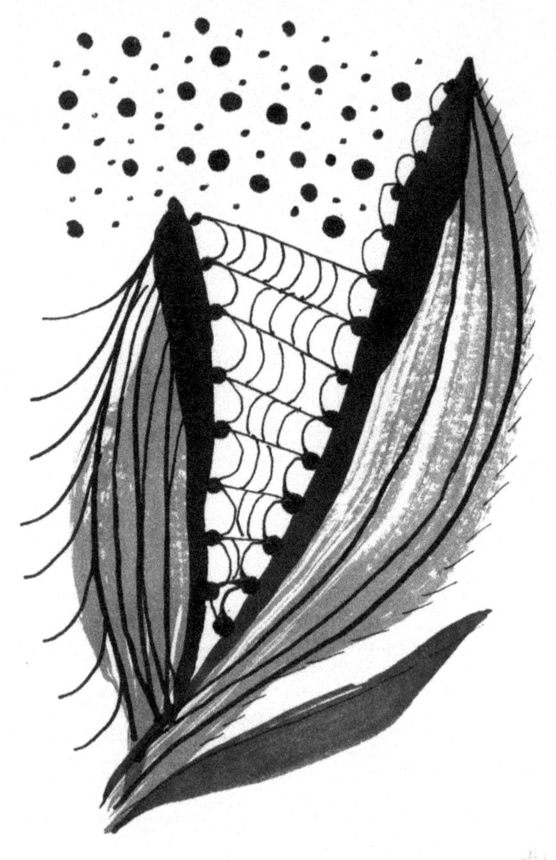

#63: What we emit, what we open to, what gets caught on a branch or root protruding from the riverbank in our heart, what clears the blockages, what we smile at as it floats, passing through.

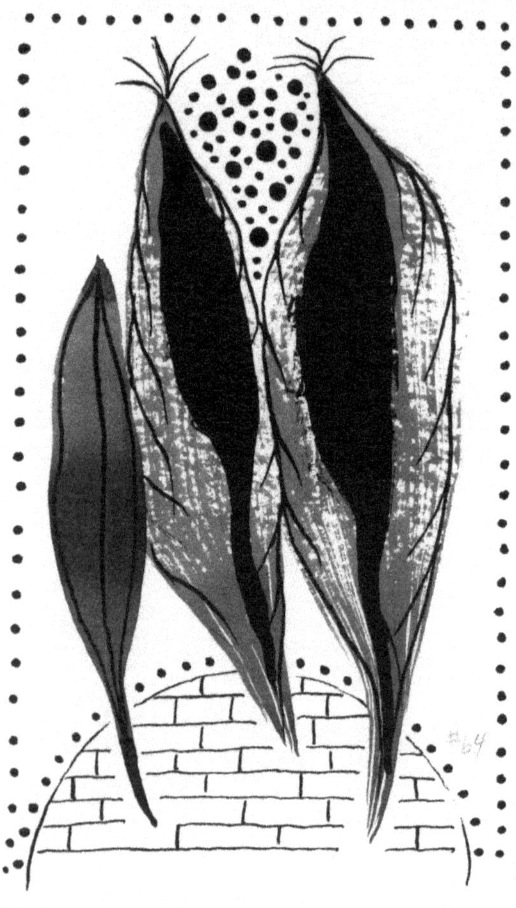

#64: Perhaps, she said, being an artist means
continuously opening inward, being willing to
discover the 7,328-plus darknesses within us—
the bats, owls, wet city streets, desires with
names like Lucinda, men in hats and long coats,
memories, roots of our ugliest, culture-driven
thoughts and our most erotic fingertips, ancient
hatreds, instructions on how best to die with
consciousness leaving through the crown
fontanels or perhaps the left nostril—and to let
those darknesses walk, fly, bleed, feed their way
to our conscious minds or our brushes and pens
so that our entire bodies become intricate root
systems where words and images travel along
darkened and illuminated arteries and veins and
we become utterly alive, recognizable as such
once every so often by another member of our
tribe, often not, occasionally sensed in general as
different, mainly because of the antennalike
energy growing out of our heads and the
murmurations of small black birds and intricate
ideas that gather in the sky in our vicinity.

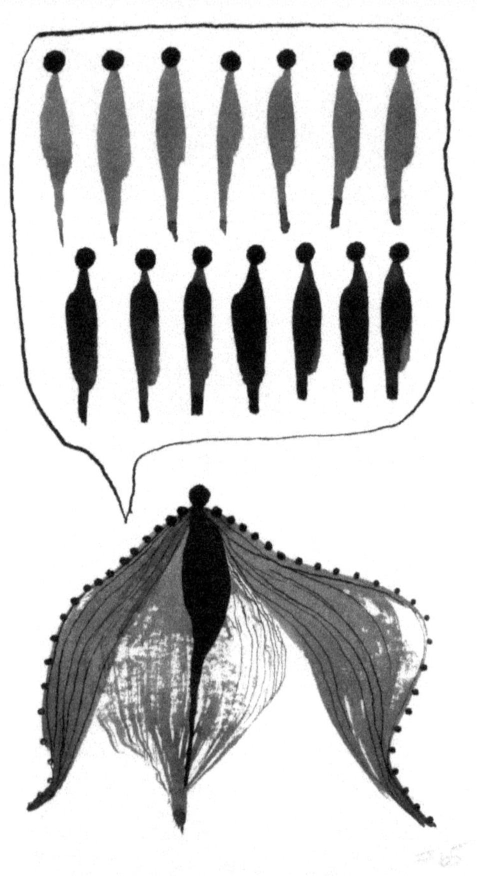

#65: And then there are nights, she said, when
we rise, each of us, moonward, feeling, with Walt
Whitman, that we contain multitudes.

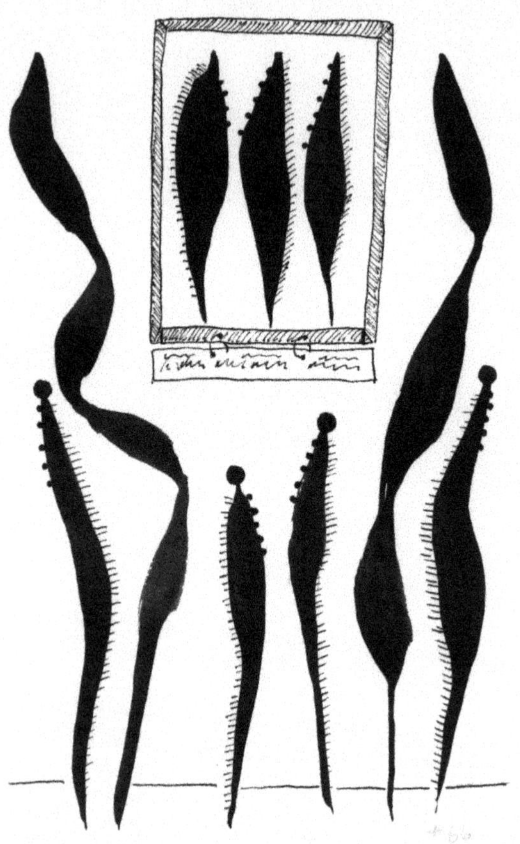

#66: When you find people inside of you, some of them talk, and some just carry things, like a lemon or one of those old black metal lunchboxes; others have sensors all over their exoskeletons and attend art exhibits, where they are astonished to see, reflected in the art, elements of their own inner lives.

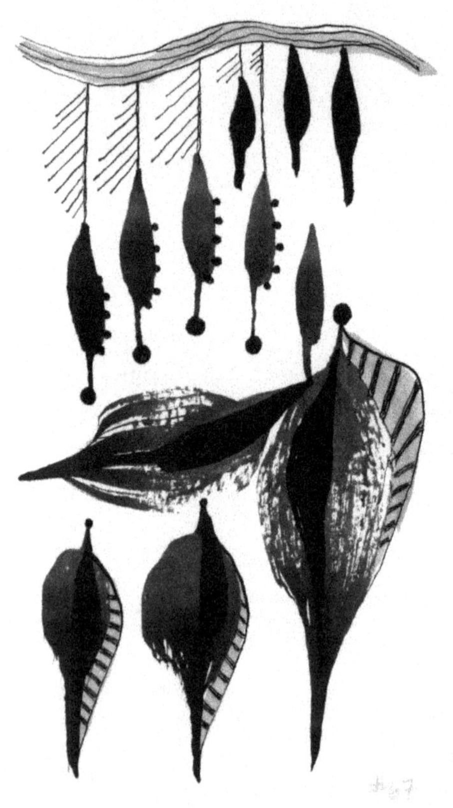

#67: Some (of the people inside you) dangle like resting bats inside your cranium, some rise from your foot soles up through your ankles and grow wide, filling up your calves and shins.

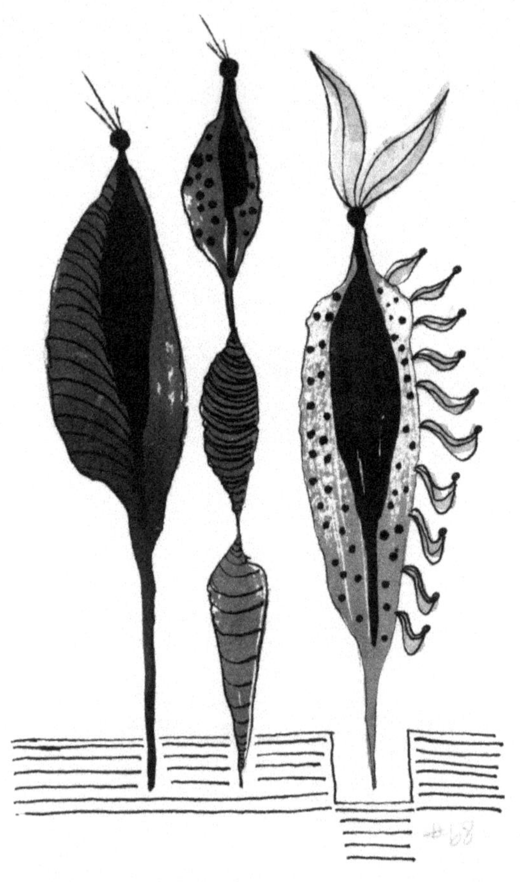

136

#68: To picture the Tao in the world, you think,
picture a stream and the sea, or yourself as the
carrot, the turnip, the lily, the milkweed or
millipede you recognize within.

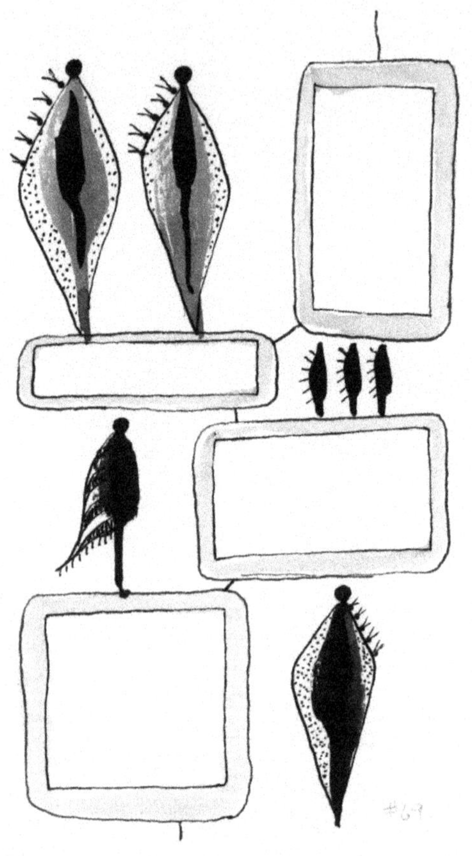

#69: Or stand someplace, any place really, alone
or accompanied, for as long as it takes to begin
to feel your tendrils reaching forth, seeking, and
while you're there, tune in to what travels in and
out through your outermost membrane, sensing
if possible the direction in which the particles
are flowing, and check whatever's available in the
external world to see if you can see what's
reflected back.

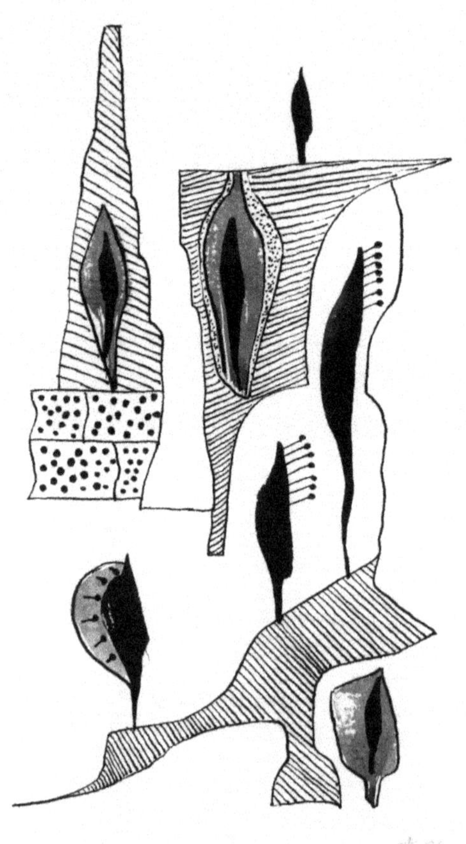

#70: And then, by accident, you catch the world
from just the right angle, and you see abundant
openings that weren't apparent moments
before—invitations, eminences, imarets,
incarnadine passages out of which emergences
feel imminent.

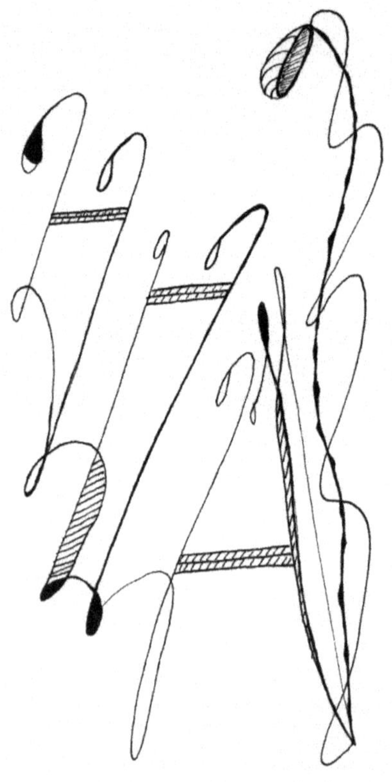

#71: There was a man some place, whistling, and Edna told me that when a woman she knew heard the notes, she saw them writing their way in wiry light across the night sky, the beauty of which caused her to stand in one spot so long she became convinced that she was made of stars stitched together by the threads of music, and to this day no one's been able to talk her out of it.

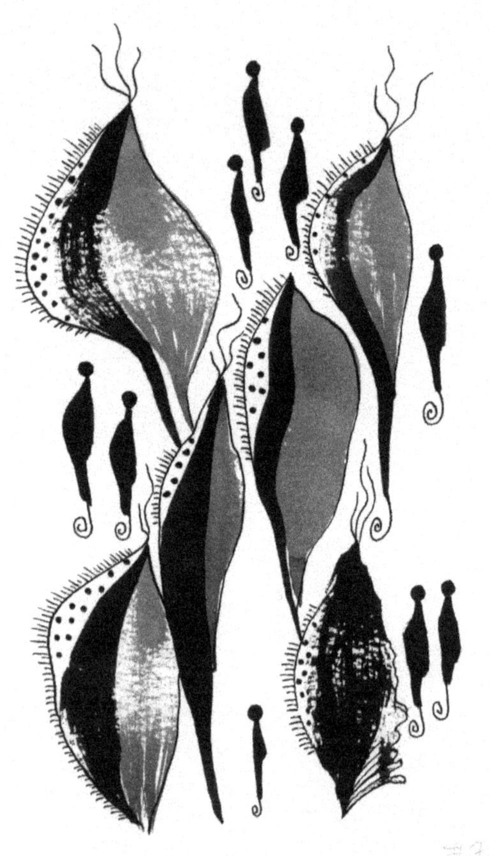

#72: On Thursday, Eliza accepted an invitation to meet in the arboretum and move very slowly from place to place, receiving her direction from the trees.

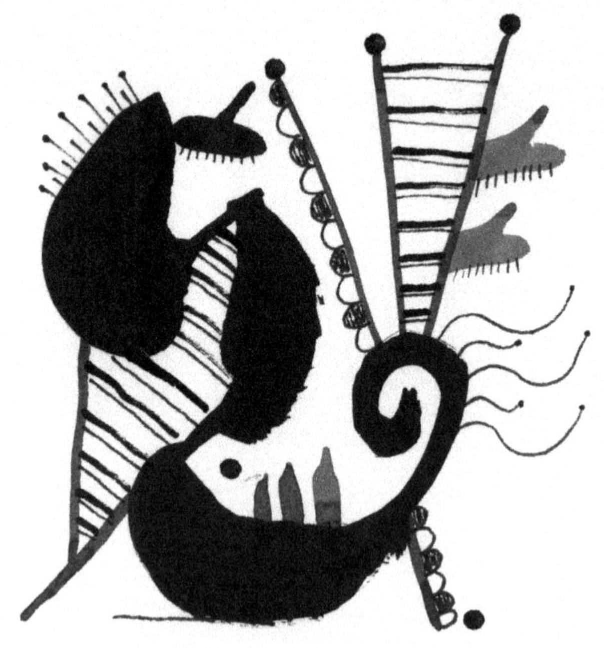

146

#73: It is possible, Mr. Leopold said to no one in particular, to make of one's mind a musically enhanced playground of endless delights if one commits to reading certain combinations of unusual books.

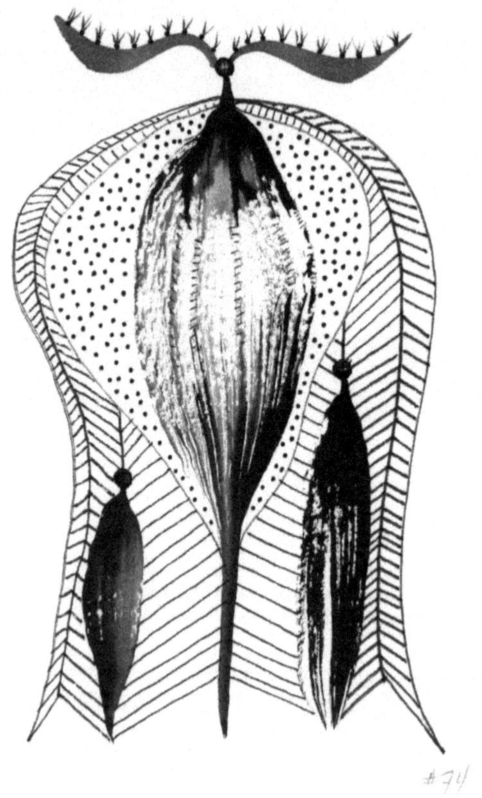

#74

#74: Do you remember that time, Mr. Leopold
asked Henrietta, when we'd both been reading
Proust, Mary Ruefle, and "The Tibetan Book of
the Dead," and we met in a dream under the
skirt of an eminent being, but we couldn't tell if
we were about to encounter peaceful or wrathful
deities, the shrunken heads of our family
members arranged neatly in an egg carton,
or a young woman we saw through a window 30
years ago, kissing another young woman?

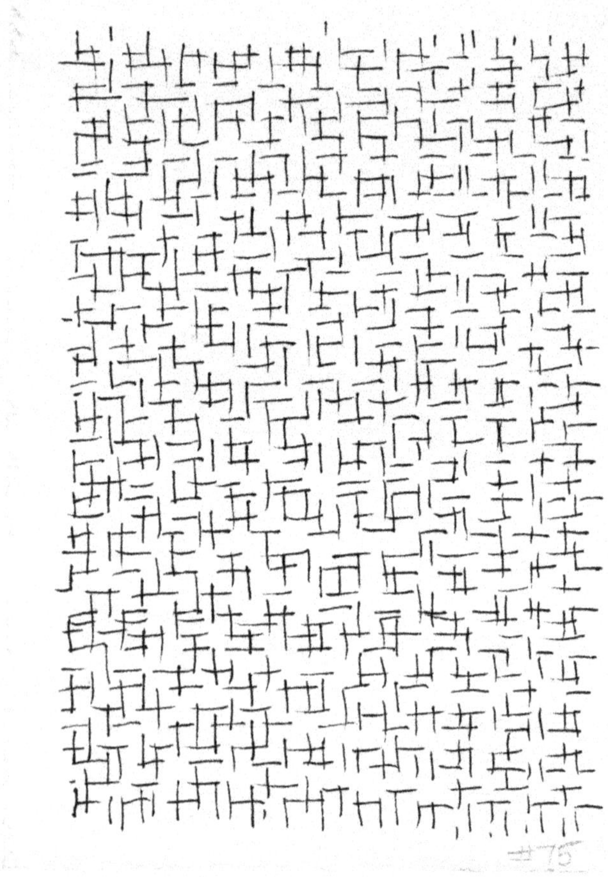

#75: Or remember that time you committed yourself to serving the spirit that spoke to you, recording meticulously what you knew were the most profound expressions on the nature of love and grief and memory and desire, but then, of course, the spirit's language was not ours, and so it became our mission to search the languages and symbols of the world until we found the key to translating what you had so devotedly channeled?

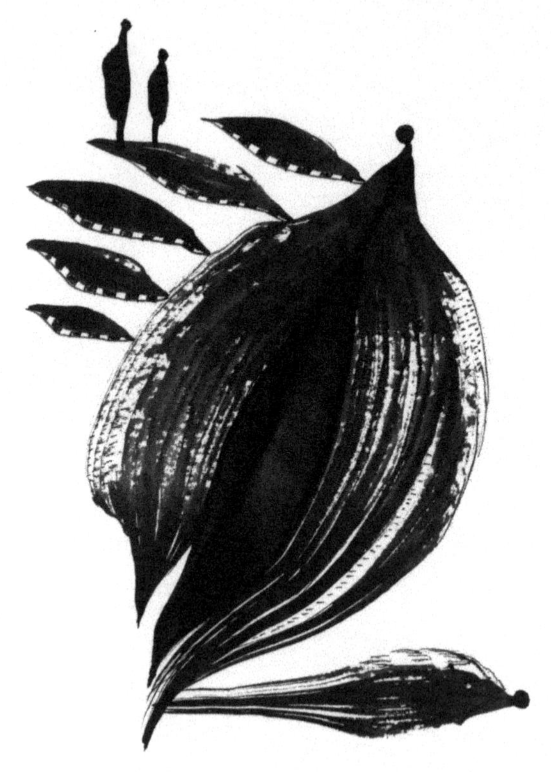

#76: Distant as we were from each other geographically, sometimes, in our devotions, we felt so close it was as though we shared a single shadow, and that shadow–like a flying carpet finely woven from impulses, sunflowers, recollections, dream images, snakes, turtles, yearnings, teacups, futures–connected us to something larger than creativity even, so we stood there together on our little patch of darkness and traveled where we were led.

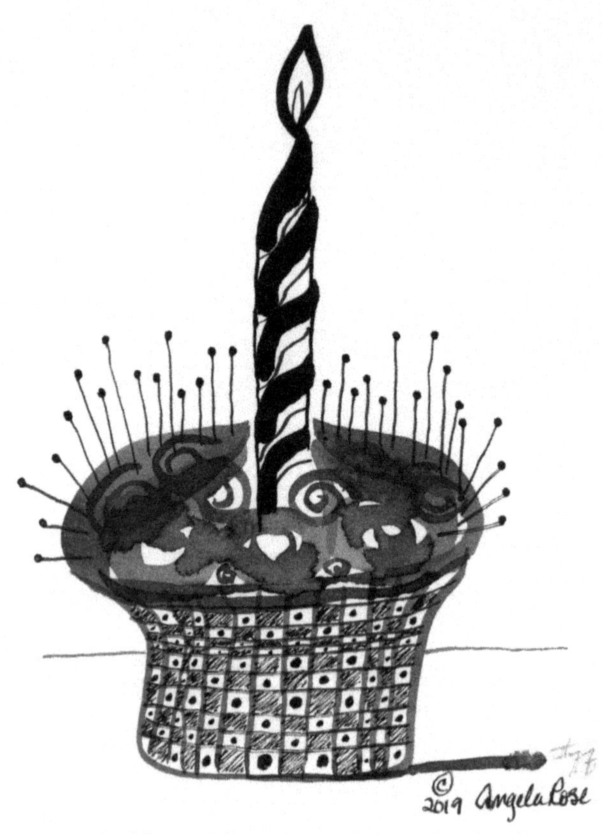

154

#77: Occasionally, we stopped, looked around, and, despite the unavoidable presence of a few elephant-sized sadnesses, we decided to celebrate having been born by performing what we called emotional acupuncture and later eating a shared cupcake, one small sweet bite at a time.

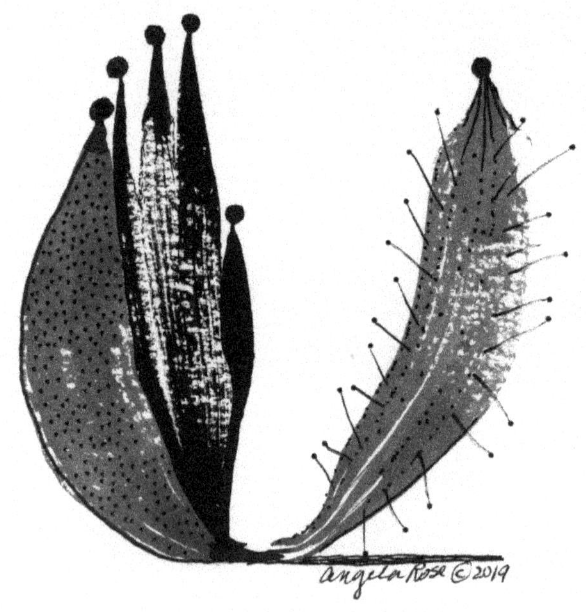

angela Rose © 2019

#78: It is impossible in such cases to read the particulars, but we knew the emotional acupuncturist had been working on Ludmilla, and since the evidence suggested that she was working through a big loss, we gathered close, emanating as much love as we could.

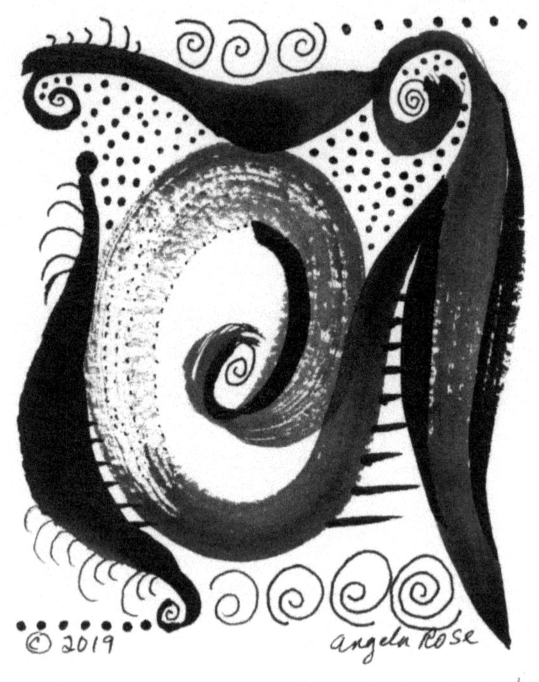

© 2019
angela Rose

#79: Our emanations lifted Ludmilla's spirits notably.

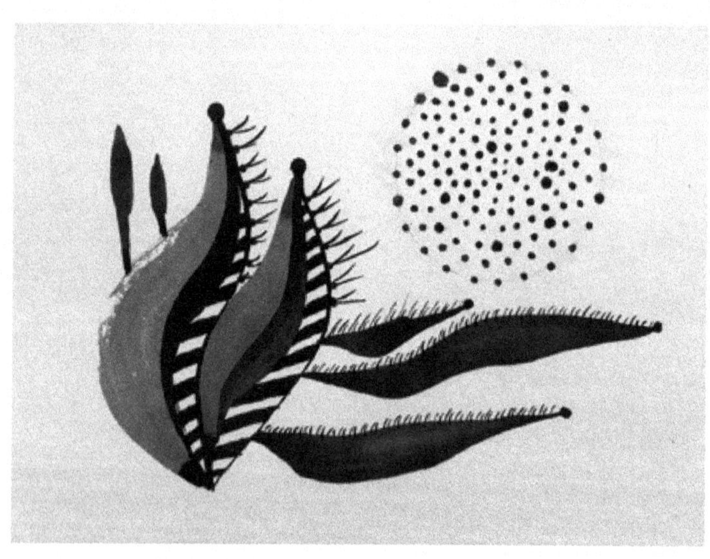

#80: So it didn't overly surprise us when we saw that, collectively, in addition to lifting Ludmilla's spirits, our emanations, which had been composed of love, kept flowing, and from that continuous flow new energetic entities formed themselves, one of which—a magnificent orb composed of ever-vibrating particles of creativity—offered itself to us as at once both bottomless question and trusted guide.

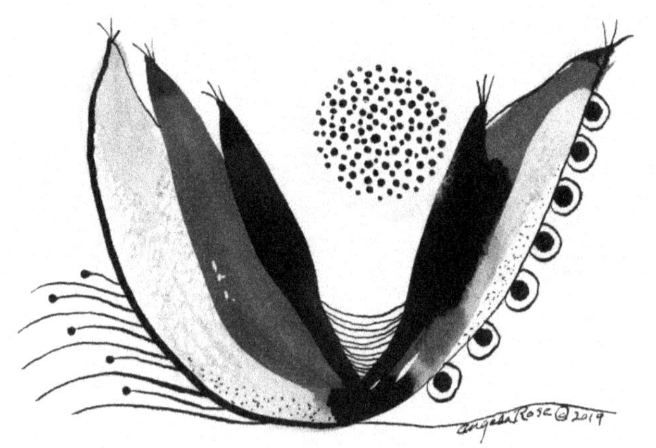

#81: Thus it was that we began a new stage of our journey together, keeping always at least one of our collective eyes open so that if we happened to notice that any among us exhibited feelings of excessive attachment, aversion, pride or envy, we would be aware that they may have fallen into the hands of the lord of death, or if one of us dreamed, between dawn and daybreak, that she was riding a cat or a monkey with a red face, we would recall that this is a sign of death caused by king spirits, and we would therefore be certain to seek and perform the proper rites for averting death, which may or may not include building an effigy.

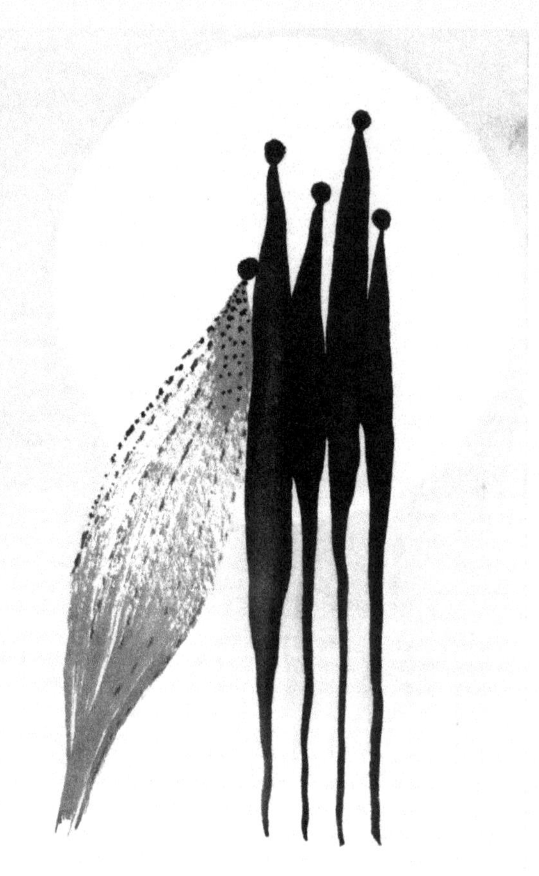

#82

164

#82: When one of us grew tired, paled, lost her
identity or baffled us with fears, we learned,
though not without much faltering, to make of
ourselves a trunk against which she might rest,
since the length of a life is a lot like the length of
a sunrise walk, and none of us wanted to miss
the pink and yellow streaking of clouds or the
great blue heron, just about to extend its
hunched neck.

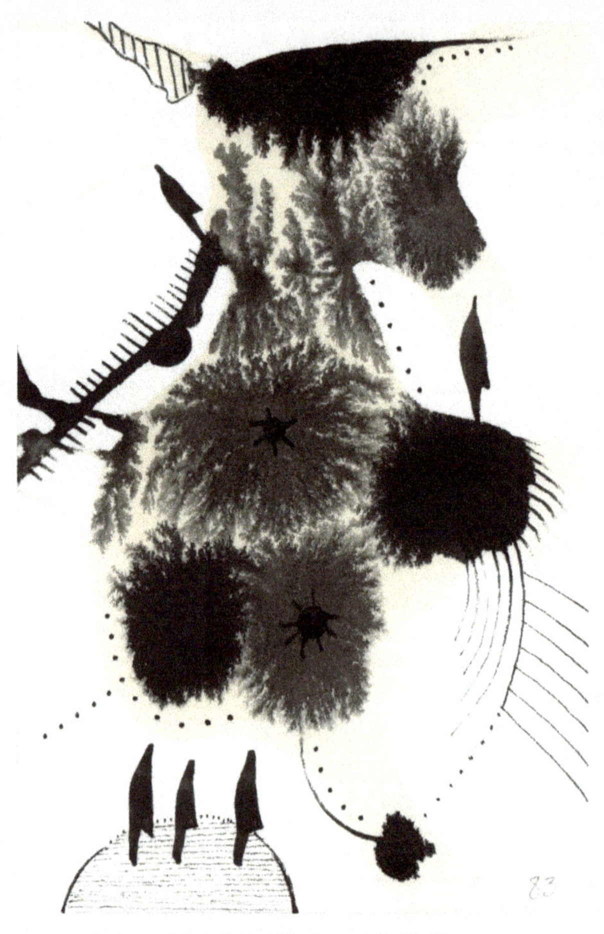

#83: A terrible explosion from within overwhelmed all our best efforts, and we struggled to accept how lost and bereft we felt.

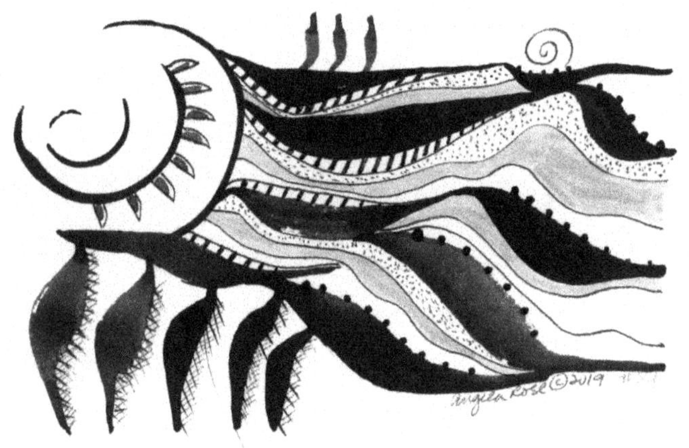

#84: Ludmilla noticed, on the distant horizon, a snail-shaped scribble of smoke, which she took to suggest that within all the complex layers competing for her attention, she could, if she created spaciousness enough within, detect her pure intention, and she could thereafter channel all of her energies in its direction.

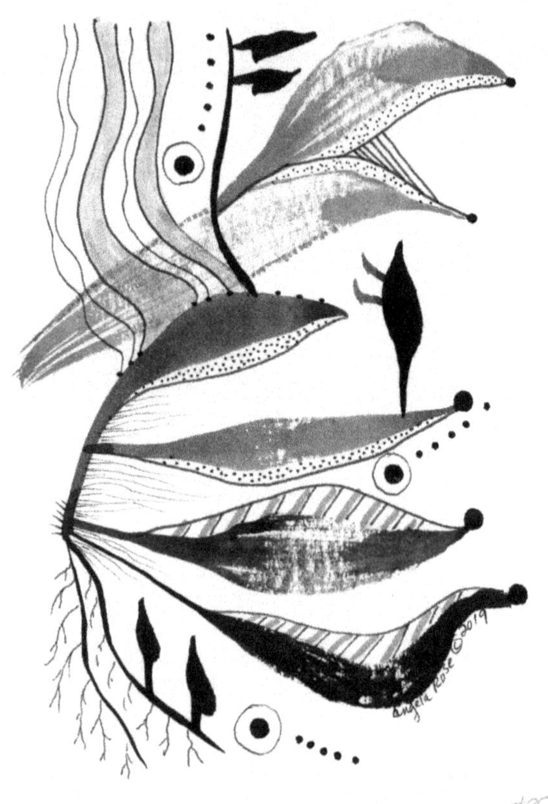

angela rose © 2019

#85: She imagined that, years from now, she might look back on this day–with its frigid winds at sunrise, its essay that she read in the sunlit den from a fat book with a green cover, its conflicts and concerns that meandered the pathways of her mind, its flickers of desire and images from a Japanese film that had stuck with her from the previous evening–and she might notice in it numerous roots and tendrils that would so obviously feed later experiences, elements she couldn't possible understand the significance of except from the remove that the passage of many years could provide, and this knowing created within her a feeling of at once curiosity and peace, a feeling she savored the taste of as she rolled it around on her tongue, mixing it in with sips of milky coffee.

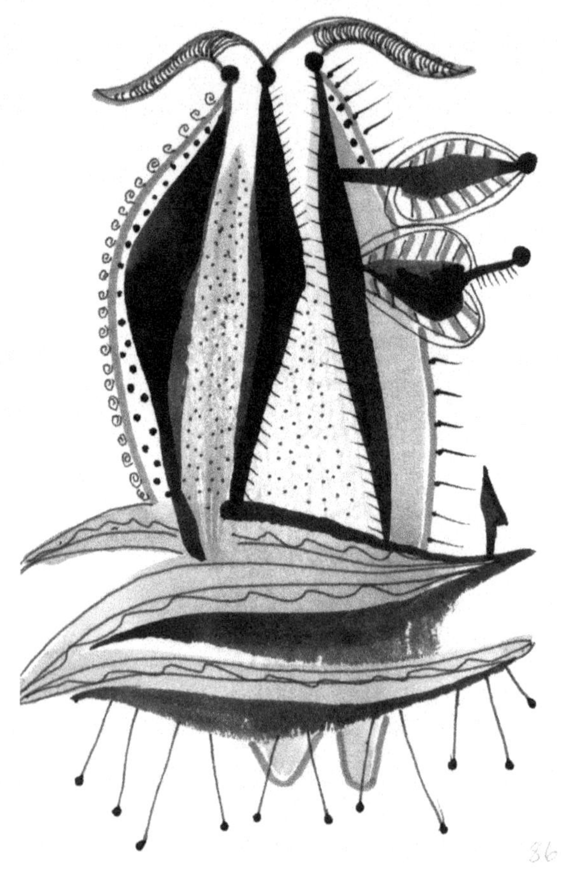

#86: That night she dreamed she was moving to another world—was it the great transition of death and possibly rebirth that she'd read about in "The Tibetan Book of the Dead"?—and she found herself on a thin slip of firm ground, from which she could see beneath her an opening, out of which emanated crashing sounds as of a distant ocean, and before and above her several powerful beings, the tallest 3 of which had bodies like ancient minarets or great redwoods that leaned so as to create two possible entryways.

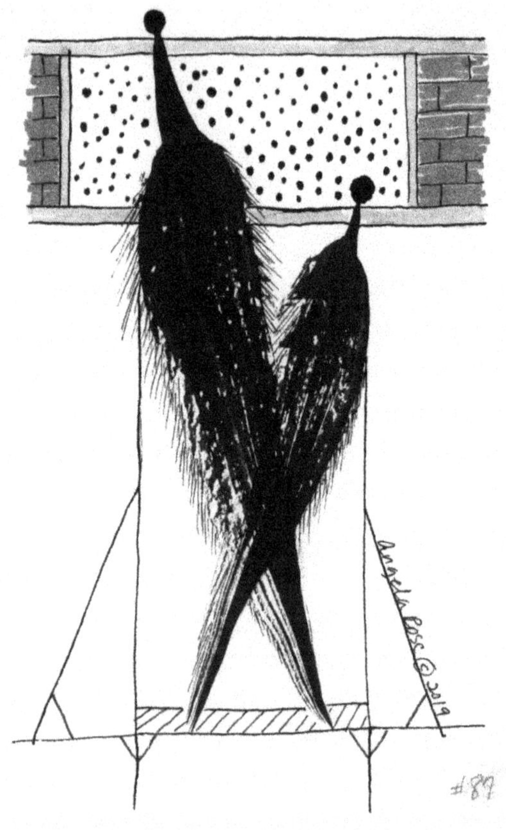

#87: When she stepped through the entryway on the right, she found herself beside her old friend, the two of them standing on a bit of makeshift scaffolding, neither of them able to speak as they looked out on thousands of birds, all of them traveling where it was their nature to travel.

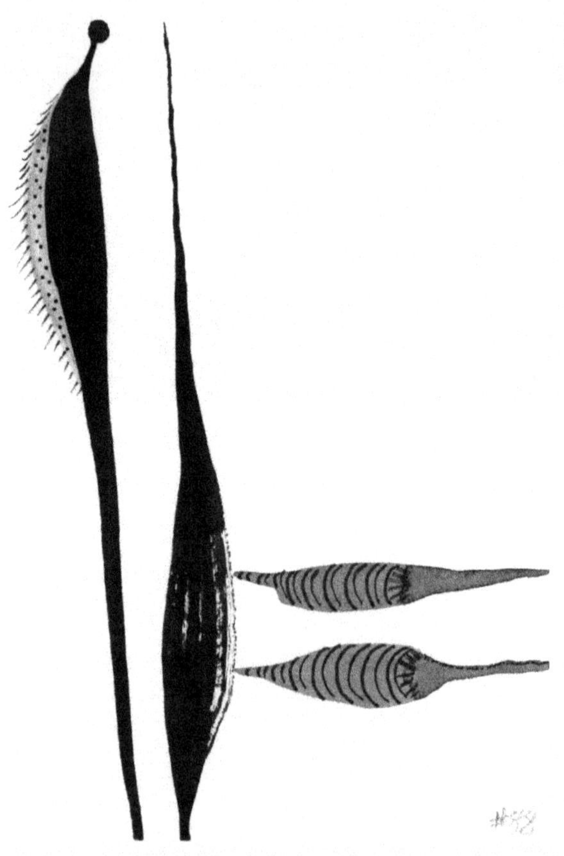

#88: She stood there, feeling layer upon layer the desolation of a particular goodbye.

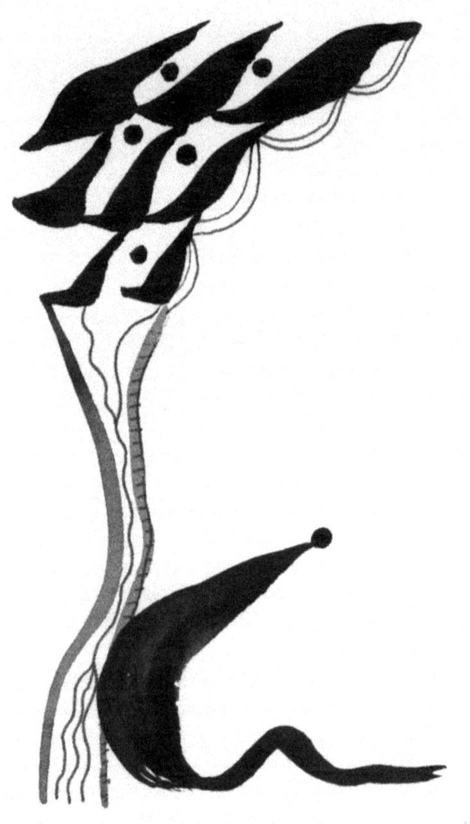

#89: One could collapse from heartbreak, she thought, or one could take one's body, heart included, to rest at twilight under a tree where large birds roost and are difficult to count in the elusive glow.

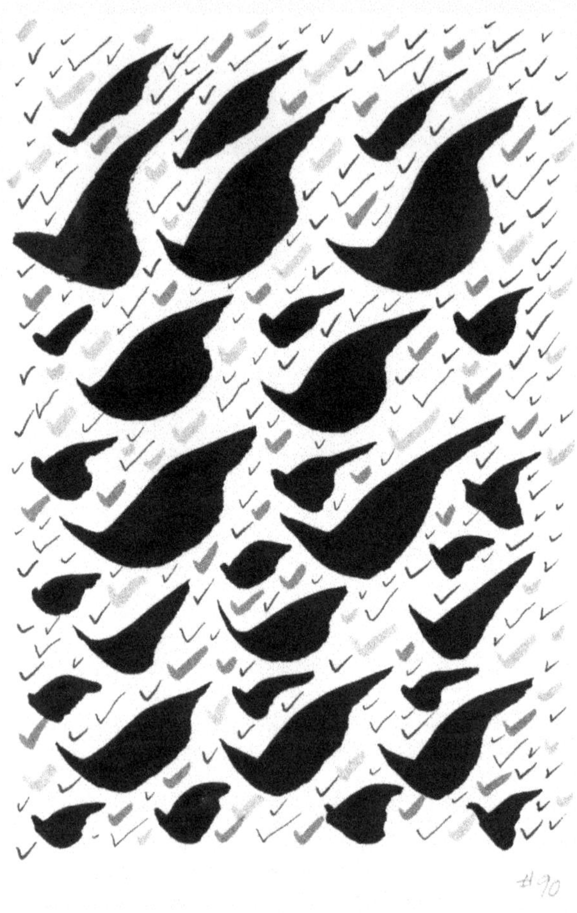

#90: Or she could breathe the hinges of her heart wide open and watch as an entire deluge of birds, wave after wave after wave of uncountable wings, whooshed through.

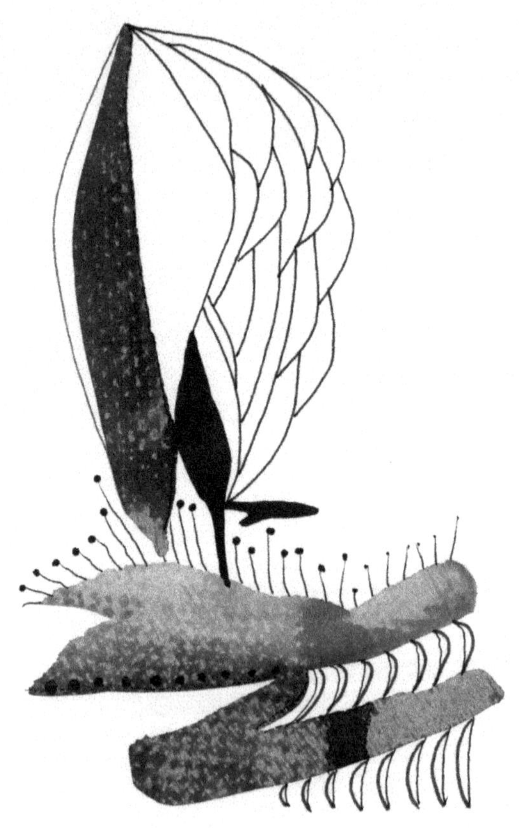

182

#91: She found that, in the aftermath of opening, when the last of thousands of wings of thousands of birds had flown through her heart, taking with them all the dead leaves, gnarled roots and even a few stray teeth that had been cluttering it, the ground on which she stood felt particularly animate, as if it had legs of its own, and she knew she need only align herself with its direction, and trust in its assistance on her journey.

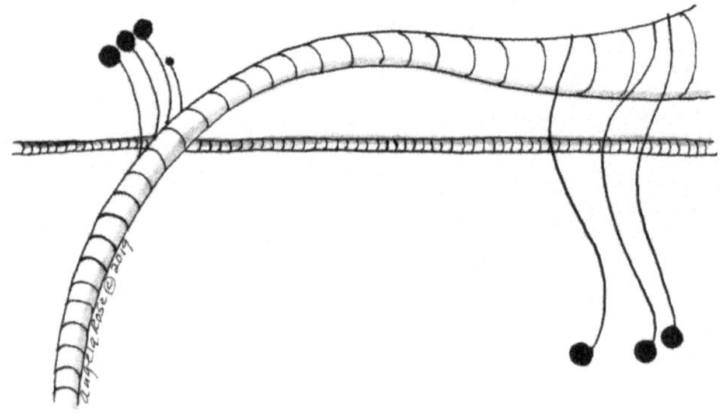

184

#92: But the ground beneath one's feet, in a land one has just awakened to, is a subtle thing, especially when it has feet of its own, so she stood still, knowing that she might need to listen for a long time, might need to swallow several small moons, one waning crescent at a time, in order to determine the precise and meandering direction in which to travel.

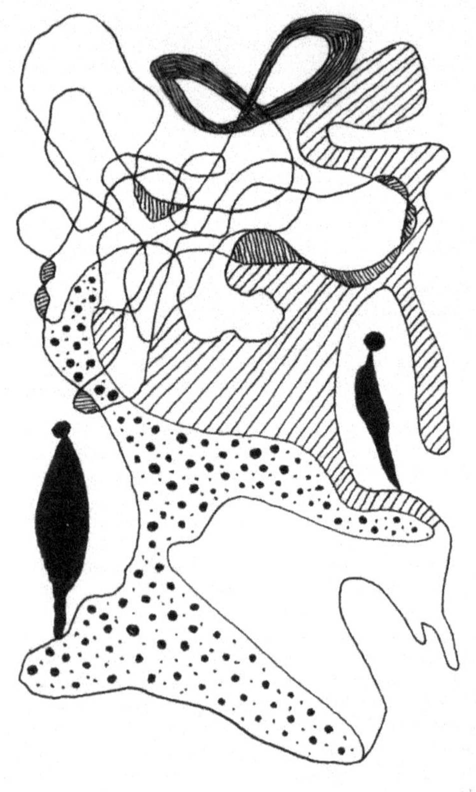

#93: When she listened deeply enough, she
realized she had a friend, not far away, though
distance between humans, she thought, with its
tangled, circuitous, and knotted interior and
exterior geographies, is something not
easily measured.

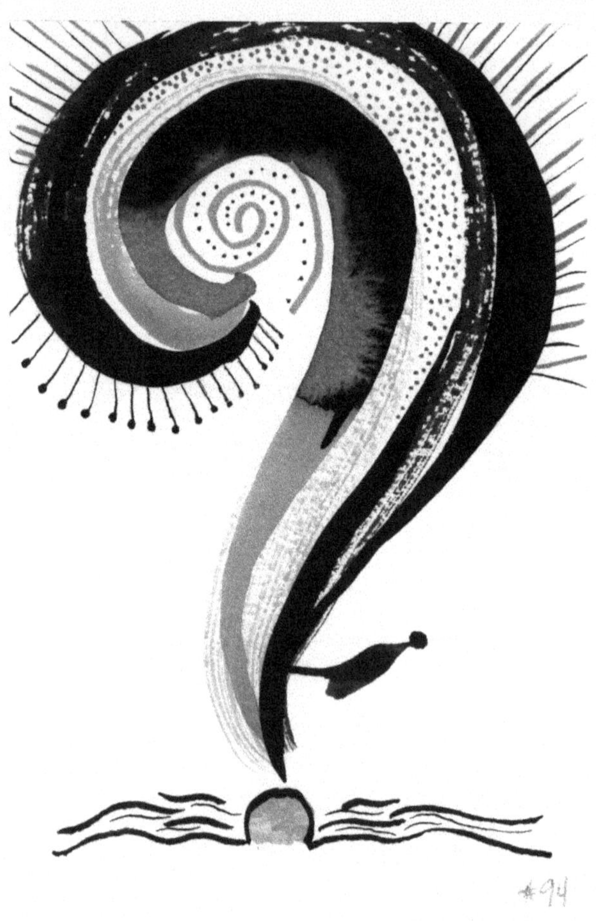

#94: At the moment, she found herself caught on a wave of deep and wide unknowing, its shape familiar, its center attractive—spiraled, filled with light–its back steep, its emanations powerful, and she decided she'd just need to ride it, walk it, breathe it, chew it, taste it, roll it around in her fingers, let its layers wash her hair and rinse her thoughts, trusting all the while that she wouldn't be destroyed in the process.

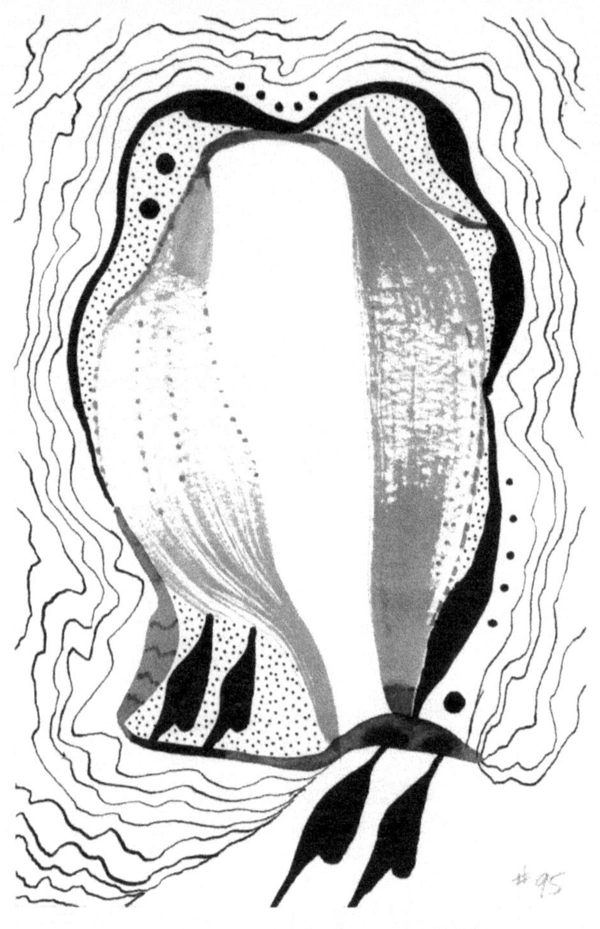

#95

#95: One thing you learn, she thought, when you travel with a shadowy companion along alternative routes, is that openings generally foretell discovery, and that, while the light beyond any threshold may suck you towards it with a force like gravity, it is worth taking time to examine the markings surrounding any opening, since they often include symbols that denote the meaning of all you are leaving behind or all you are about to encounter.

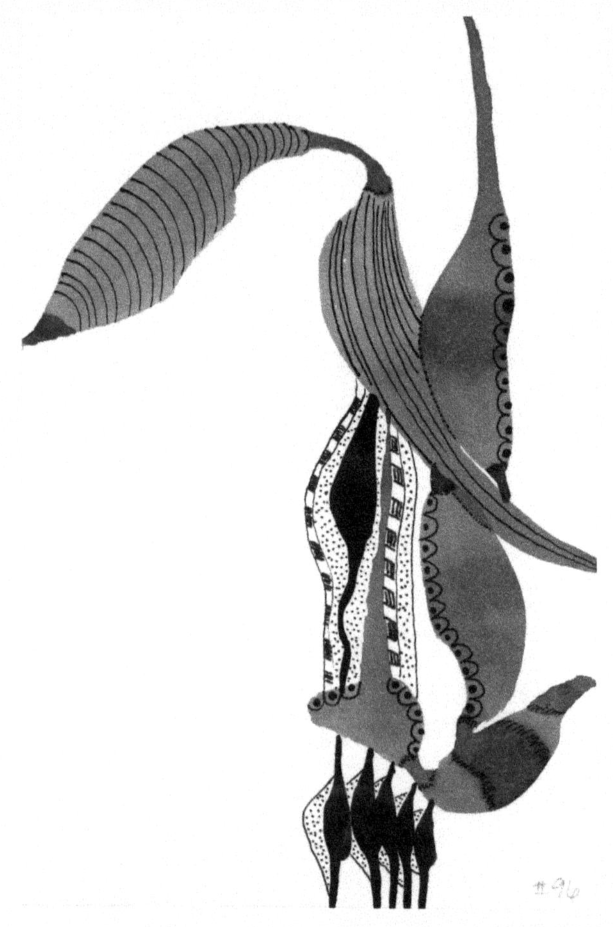

192

#96: There are moments when, after years of
practice, it becomes possible to see, rising like
billowy banners or great plumes of detailed
smoke from the tops of the heads of those one
encounters, the shapes of particular desires,
inspirations, ideas in the process of forming
themselves, or dakinis dancing in the realm of
pure awareness.

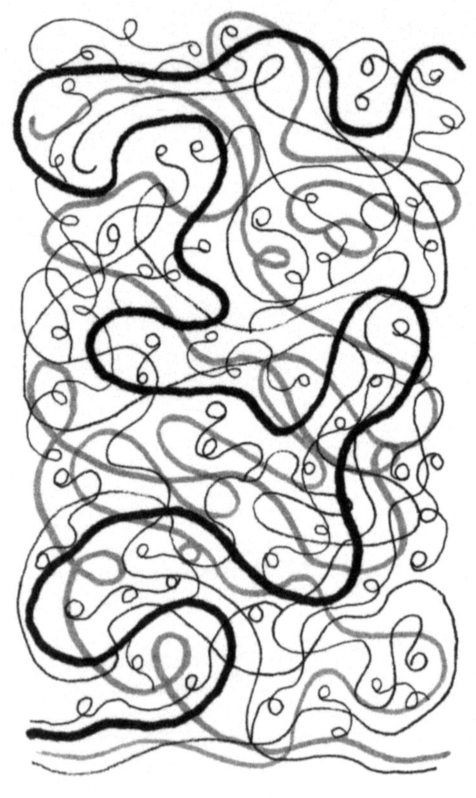

#97

#97: She went for a long walk alone in the icy snow-lit, bird-murmurating, bufflehead-brightened, early sunset of mid-December, remembering step by step and breath by breath how she'd loved a woman once and how that love had been thread shaped, string shaped, stream shaped, sea shaped, bread shaped, boiled egg shaped, tea cup shaped, soup shaped, breath shaped, book shaped, flame shaped and whisper shaped, leg shaped, skin shaped, shin shaped and finger shaped, linger shaped, hunger shaped, ache shaped and swim shaped, sand shaped, sunrise shaped, walk shaped, tree shaped, teeth shaped, grief shaped, dead oak leaf shaped, thief shaped.

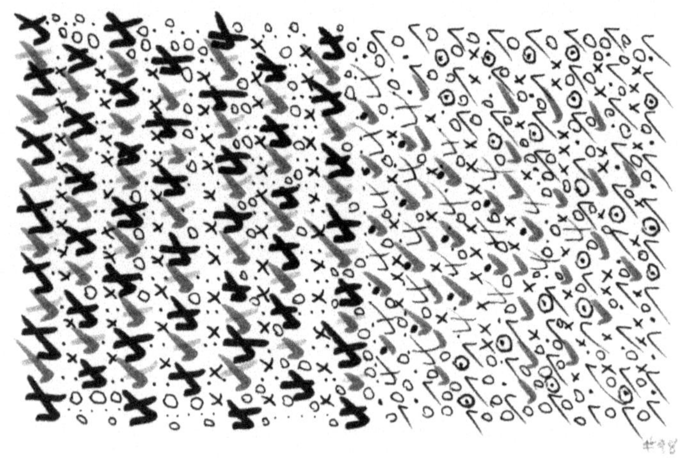

#98: She smiled at how the mind sometimes sparkles.

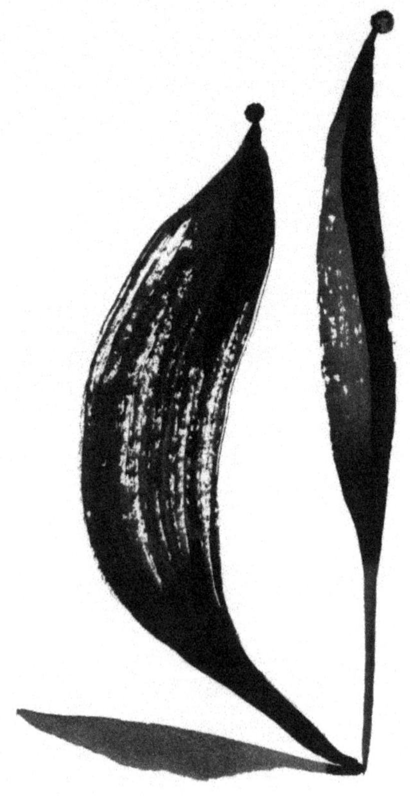

#99: Occasionally she, who was always really two—herself and her companion (even when they wore only one hat or chewed with a single set of teeth)—stopped inside a moment as under an umbrella and thought, there are actually always three participants in this conversation, you and me and our collective shadow, that unknowable dark within and between us, the part that will tell us what to do next.

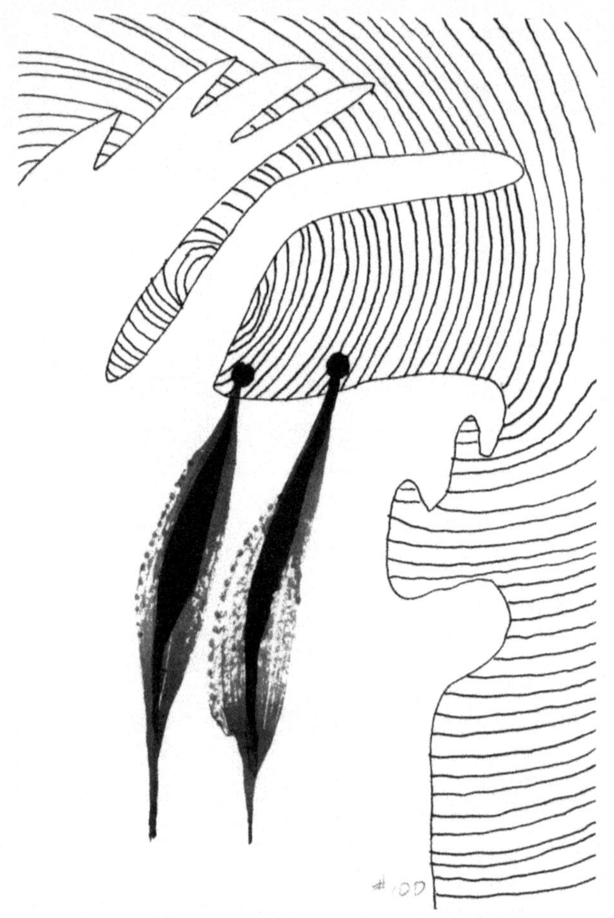

200

#100: They tried to peer into the future, and while they got the sense of something big, it was difficult to tell if they found themselves inside the barrel of a wave without a surfboard, or if they stood at the beginning of a tunnel of endless possibilities, one of which involved being absorbed into the life of a sequoia, experiencing rootedness, a new relationship to time and fog, and the movement of hundreds of gallons of water running daily from roots to crown, the two of them becoming 2 dark particles on one of its rings, a curiosity to future dendrochronologists.

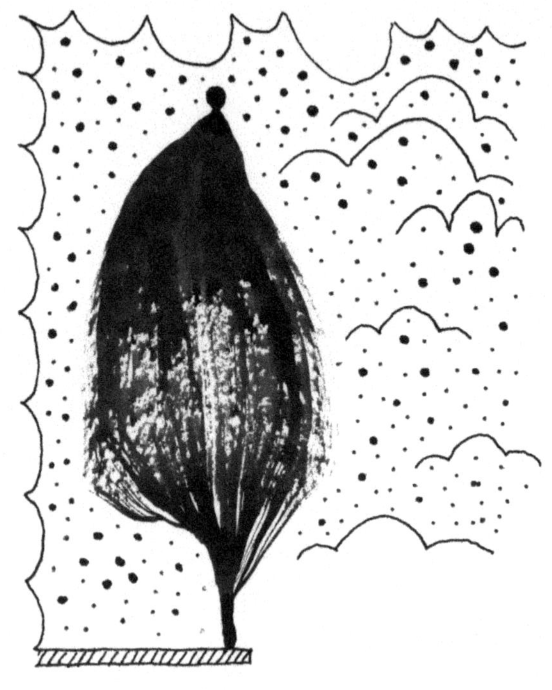

#101

#101: So she stood there, eyes closed, and let herself experience immensity and the silent, tactile language of dew and fog.

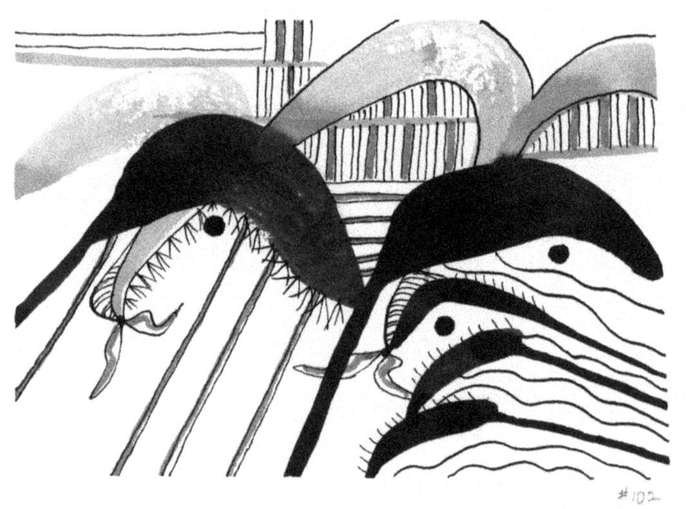

#102

#102: She learned to read messages scribbled in
tentacle and tail, in scrubby bristle and
underbelly, in mists and all things microbial.

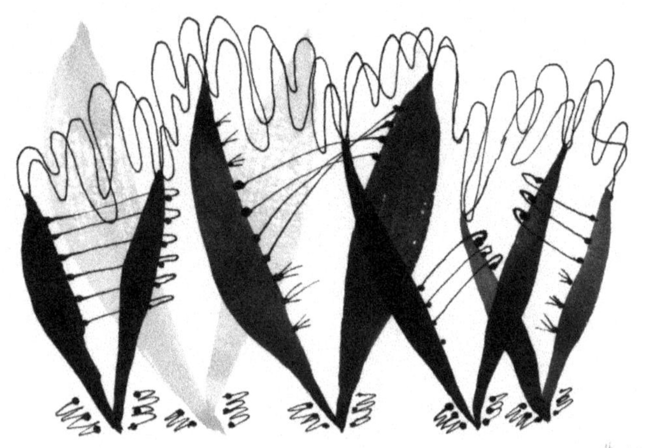
#103

#103: Elation, in that language, is represented on the page as several beings dancing in pairs, all of them connected by strands of high frequency energy running between them, the strands somewhat taut at body level, more and more wildly alive at mind height.

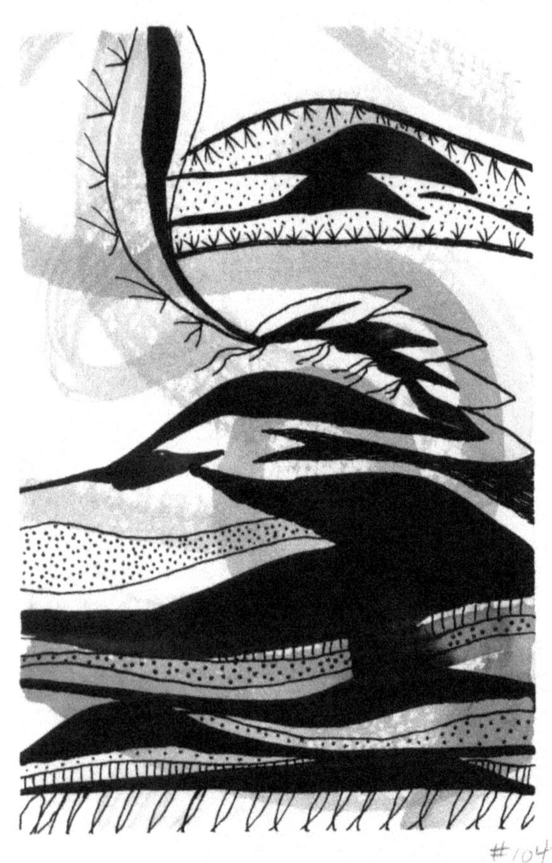

#104

#104: Conflict, she surmised, could never be accounted for with a simple symbol or two but required a complex diagram, a map, a geological cross section, a jagged narrow pass through violent weathers towards a somewhat elusive patch of more peaceful ground.

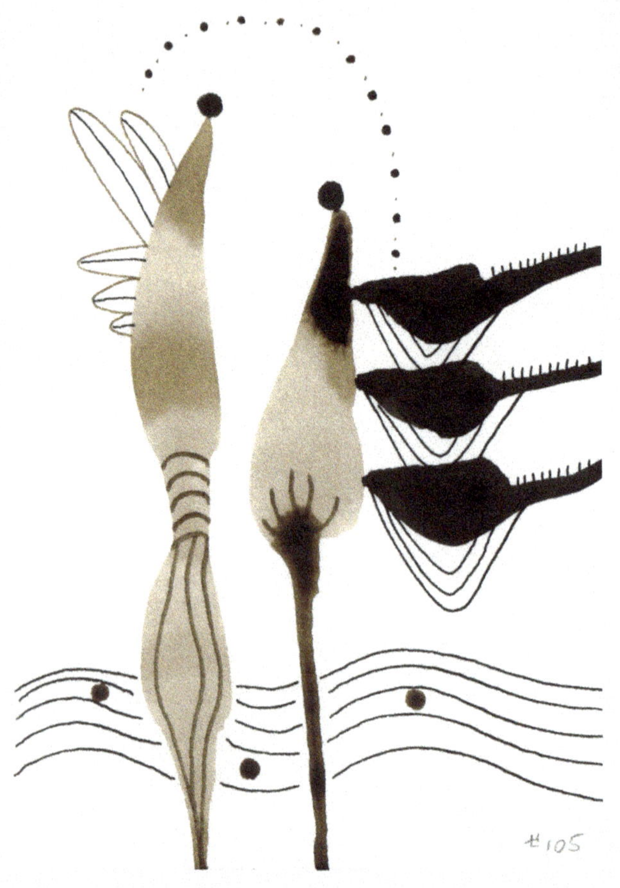

210

#105: We work, she said without speaking, because it's what we do, and because when we walk alone, which is part of the work, we don't say no to the river (made of air and skin and wind and clouds and moths and moon and music, etc.) that instructs us, even when it says, "I will gift you with eleven lonelinesses."

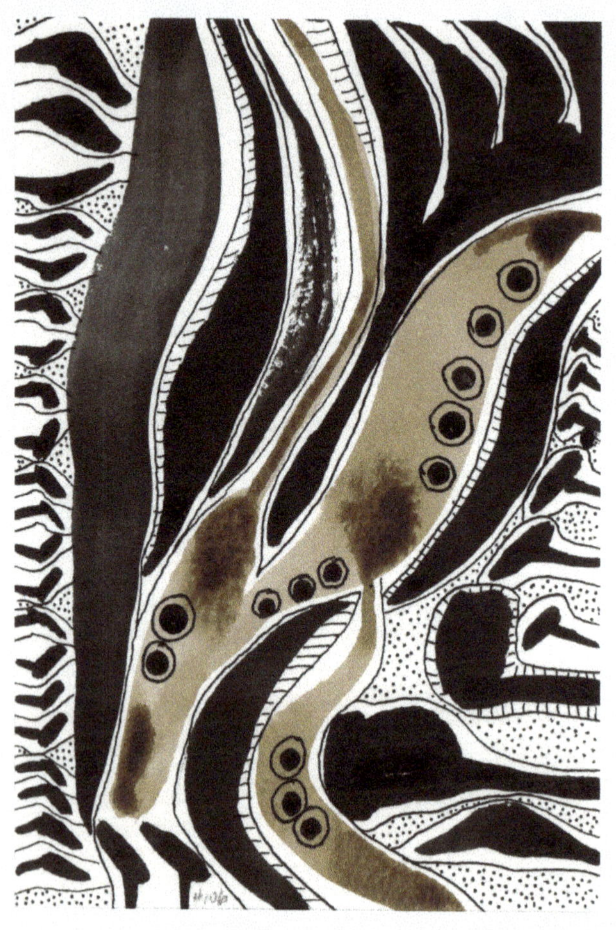

212

#106: Within a single moment inside a single loneliness is material for a several-years creation, she knew, so she began to build a first pair of socks, methodically, joyfully, in papier-mâché, listening all the while for the name of one who would fill them.

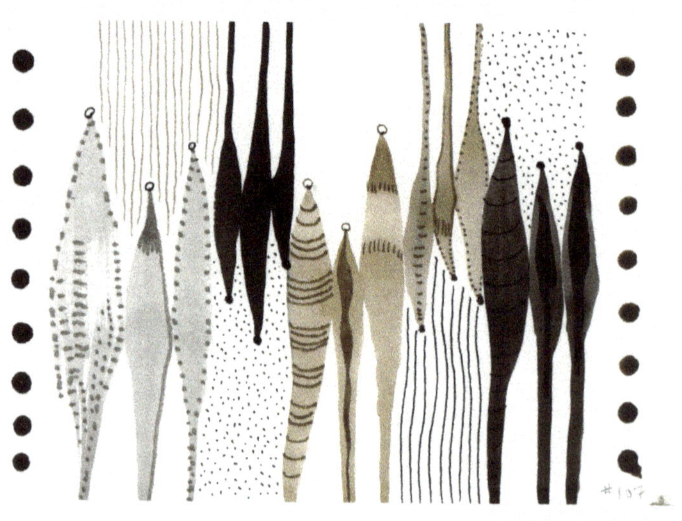

214

#107: Various characters came to her from numerous directions, some fully-clothed football-watching professionals with extended family histories, others like husks awaiting names, souls, conflicts inner and outer, and feelings one way or another for Brussels sprouts, platform shoes, roast beef, performance art, wearing seersucker etc, and yet others descended spider-like and asked her whether she'd read Kafka's very short stories, how she felt about the lack of color or descriptions of foodstuffs in Gertrude Stein's "The Making of Americans," if she knew Proust wrote much of his Search in bed in a fur coat under seven wool blankets, or that, in Japanese Noh plays, actors emerge from the world of the Dead by way of a bridge, act on the stage of the Living, and then return to the shadows by that same bridge in what Roland Barthes calls the best definition of beauty, "a scintillation between two deaths."

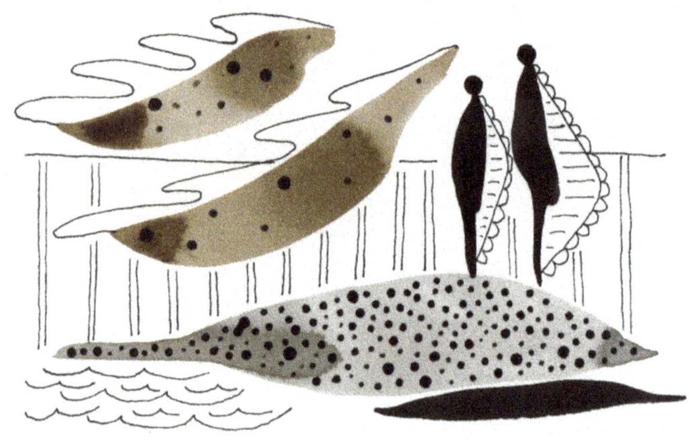

#108: It's not that one comes to expect the arrival of marvels, she thought, but one learns to recognize them.

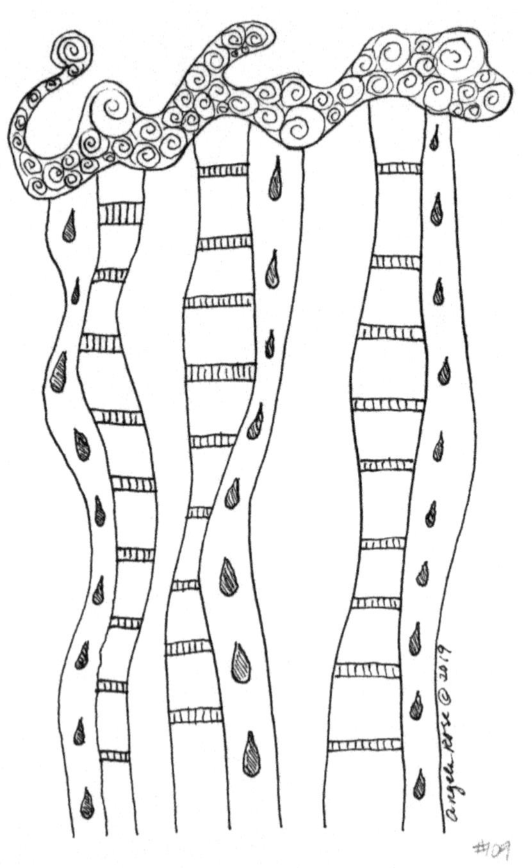
Angela Rose © 2019
#109

#109: She would set out, as such a day demands, with all of her dead in a loose orbit around her, not quite like a large hula hoop or plates she had to juggle to keep from crashing, but perhaps like musicians in an orchestra on a rotating circular stage where she, stationary in her center position even if she moved forward because she was walking, had to turn and turn and turn her consciousness to let each and every one know they were not forgotten as she walked and walked, willing one face and then another into her heart, brushing each all over with love as though love were butter and each beloved a slice of toast or roast chicken needing basting—(how one's metaphors could scramble to keep up with demands of one's mind/heart/conscience in its need to reassure the dead of their continuing significance!)—and she knew that as she walked, mile after mile after mile on the path that had once been a railroad track, eventually each of the dead would, as it were, fly off satisfied (she hoped) until next time.

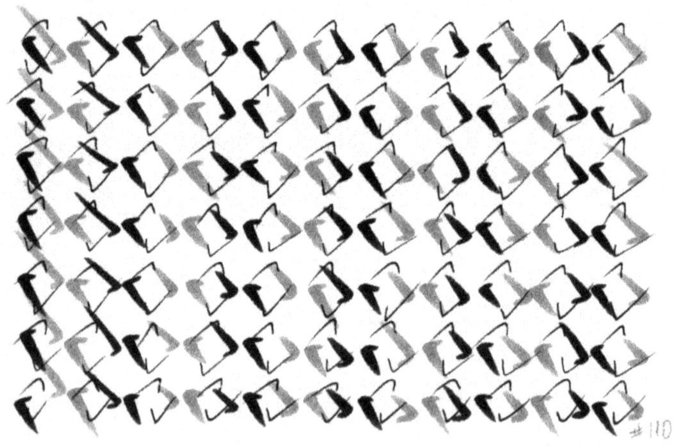

#110

#110: When the dead left, she was made entirely of windows for a pretty long while.

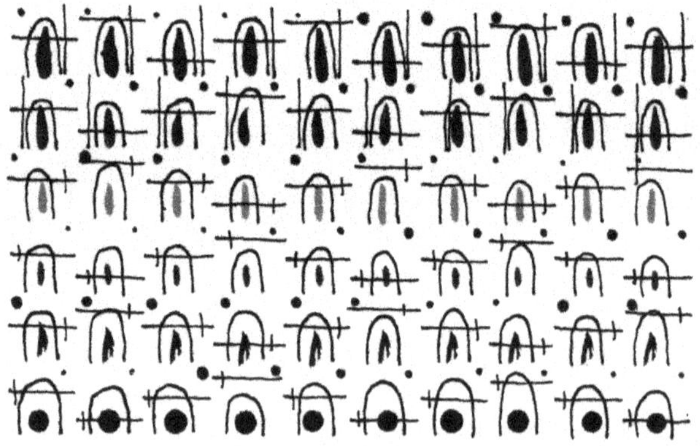

222

#111: In those days and nights when the woman was composed entirely of windows, it was sometimes possible, if one really looked at her, to see tiny flames flickering in each pane, or the moon rising, or swallows in flight, or occasionally, to catch momentary flashes of the dead, who, in their retreat, looked like thimbles of darkness against the twilight, but at other times she looked to the close observer like a cemetery on a winter morning, with all her dead locked at rest inside of her.

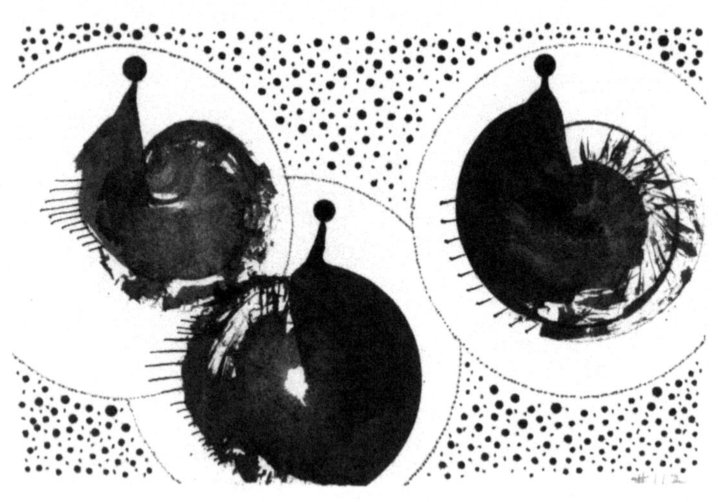

#112: For those who get very close, her intimates, who can see her from inches away or even at microscope level, there is something interstellar and galactic about her.

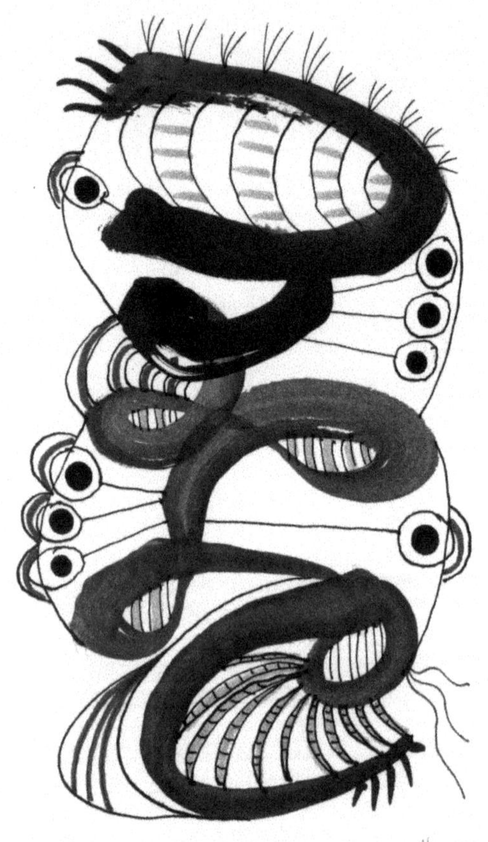

#113

#113: She had meditated long enough to recognize within her wrathful deities when they were present, but she also possessed the facility to distinguish them from beings some people might call monsters and whom she had come to know as beauty in its unfamiliar forms, this one for instance who required from her only that she run an imaginary finger along the contours of its physiognomy, counting its eyes, touching its eyelids, rubbing the scruffy little hairs that ran along its ridge, and it would relax enough to teach her the words in its language she would someday need, though when and why she would need them, it was not now her business to know.

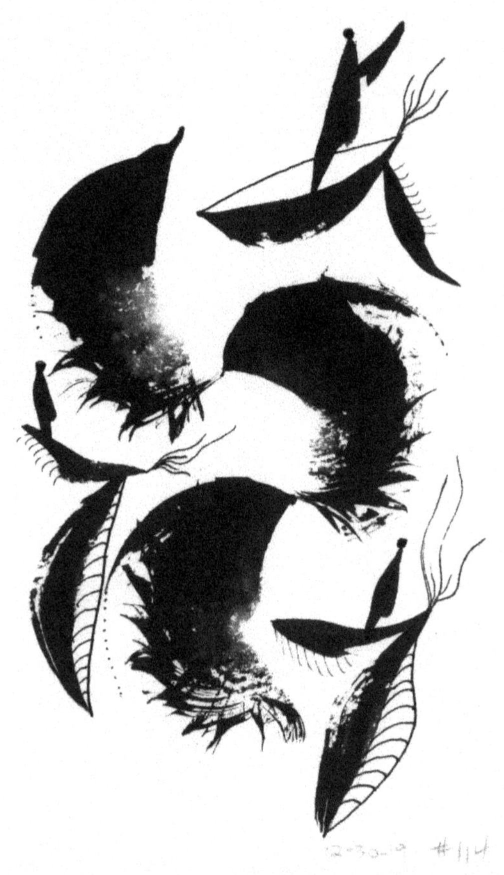

#114: Eyes closed, she could see, when she descended several flights within, the thousands of filamentary threads that held spirit to body, and she knew that she could begin, moment by moment, the many years process of snipping one thread at a time, so that when the time came, she could let go of her body's husk and fly off like a leaf in the windy sunshine.

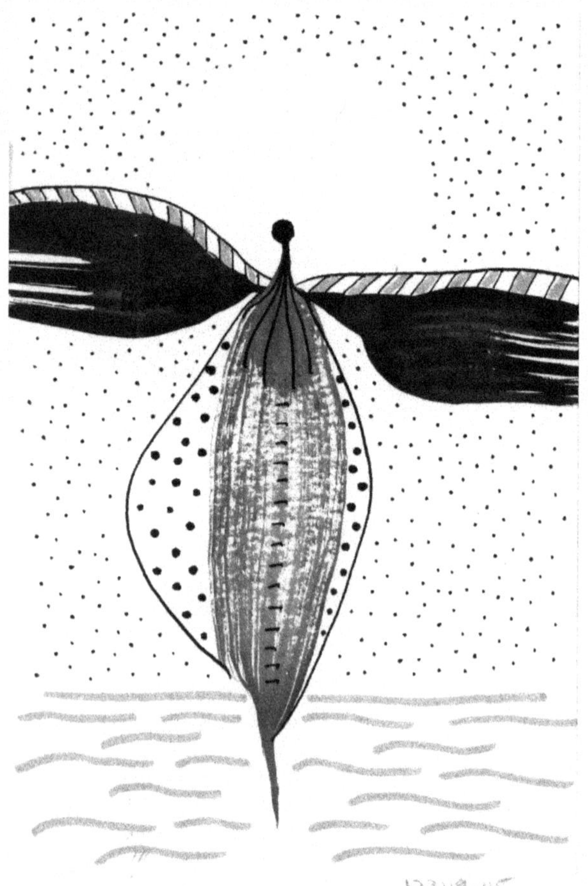

230

#115: In the meantime, she decided, she would draw, write, breathe, read, listen to old jazz, watch Japanese movies and study the translucent abdomens of luminous winged creatures.

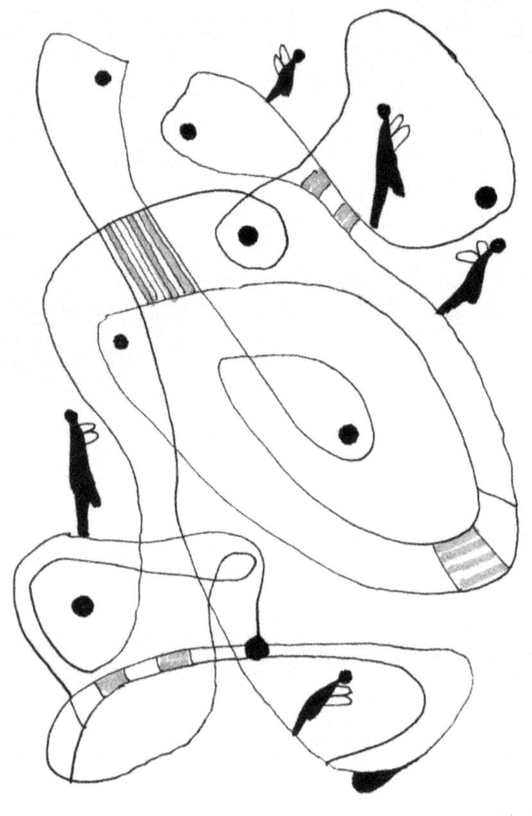

#116: It turns out there is much of delight available for study—maps, orbits, tiny winged guides, peripatetic interpreters of dreams and visions ready to offer their services for free—if only one learns to see with eyes cultivated for such particularities.

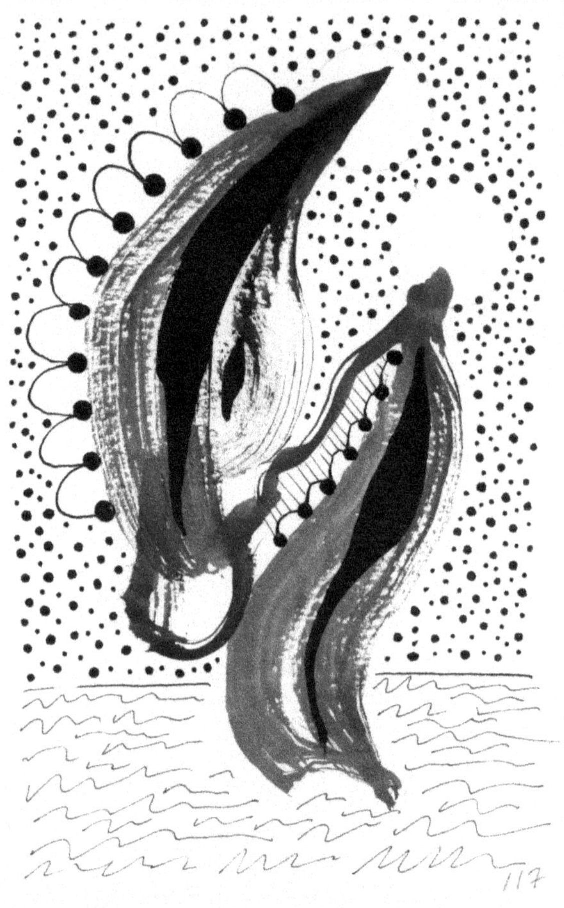

117

234

#117: In her travels she encountered some who had musical instruments embedded in their bodies—a piano-like set of keys in the dorsal portion of the thoracic area, for instance—and these beings were often accompanied by a companion who could leap and dance with exceptional expressiveness and élan.

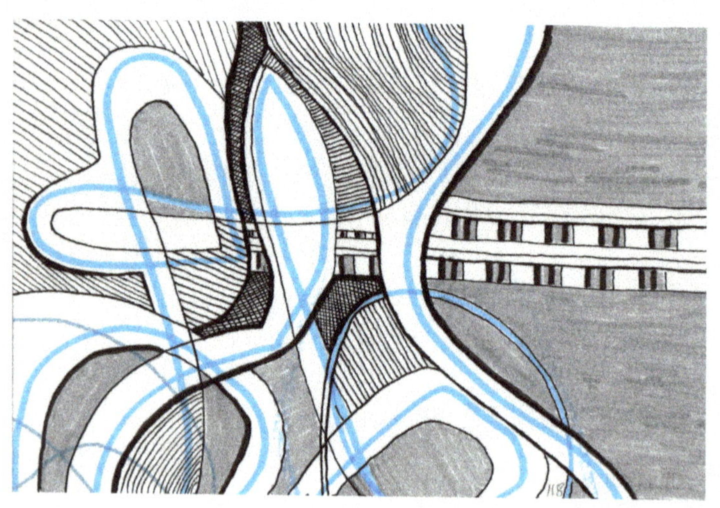

236

#118: If it were possible to so internalize music
as to have a piano-like instrument inside one
like an additional bodily organ, and if, until
recently, and then somewhat by accident and not
without an initial degree of disbelief, she had
never noticed this, nor the effect the music from
such an instrument could have on a dancer, what
other wonders had conventional expectations led
her to overlook or miss completely, and how
could she train her eyes to see more and more
truly, in the beings she encountered regularly, the
tracks and tendrils and orbs and energies
running in and out and crisscrossing in
seemingly empty air everywhere?

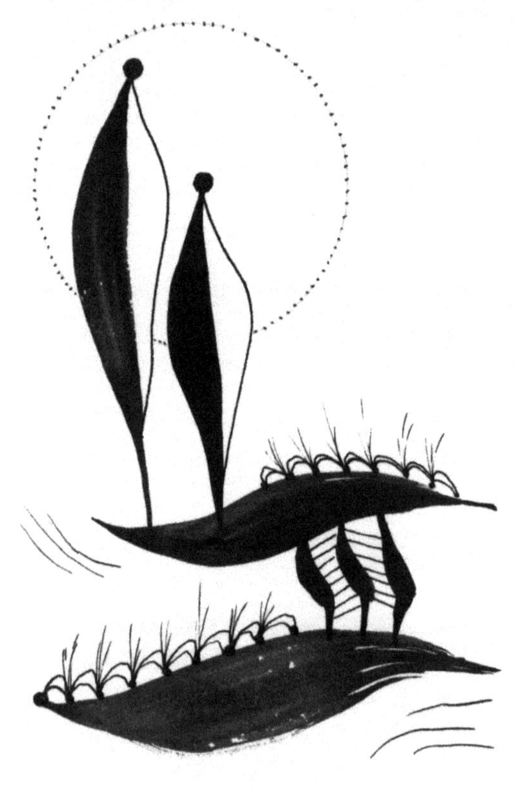

238

#119: On Tuesday, two perfectly balanced moments sped past, maintaining an orb of centered stillness within the speed at which they traveled.

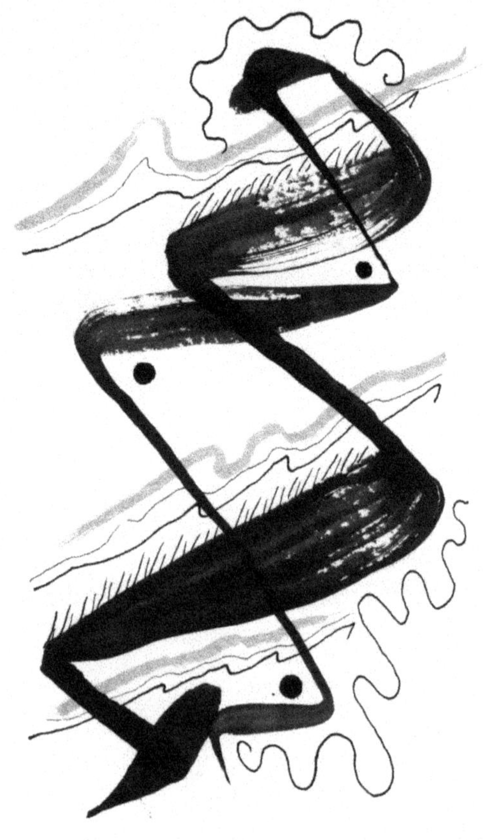

#120: On Wednesday, she stood out under the winter sky at sunrise, breathing open a river through her chest, and watched as a flock of great black birds erupted overhead.

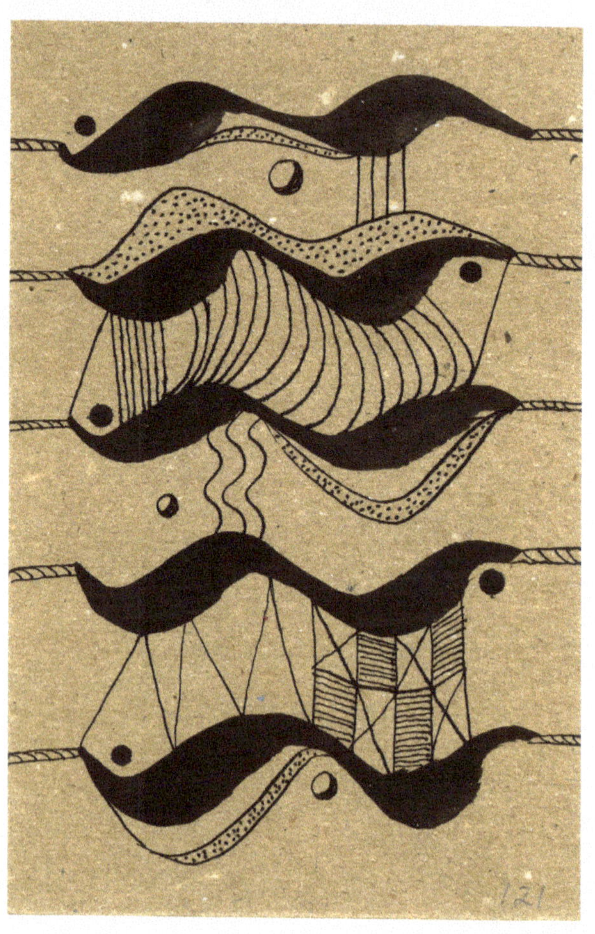

#121: On Thursday, discovering that Roland
Barthes came up with the word diaphoralogy to
denote a science of nuance and shimmerings,
and the word nuance comes from the old French
nuer, meaning "to compare shades of color to the
play of light in the clouds," she understood that,
through steady practice, that was what she was
becoming, a diaphoralogist, learning to detect, as
well as nuance and shimmerings, the subtle
architectures in the spaces between birds in a
fight of sparrows or unkindness of ravens.

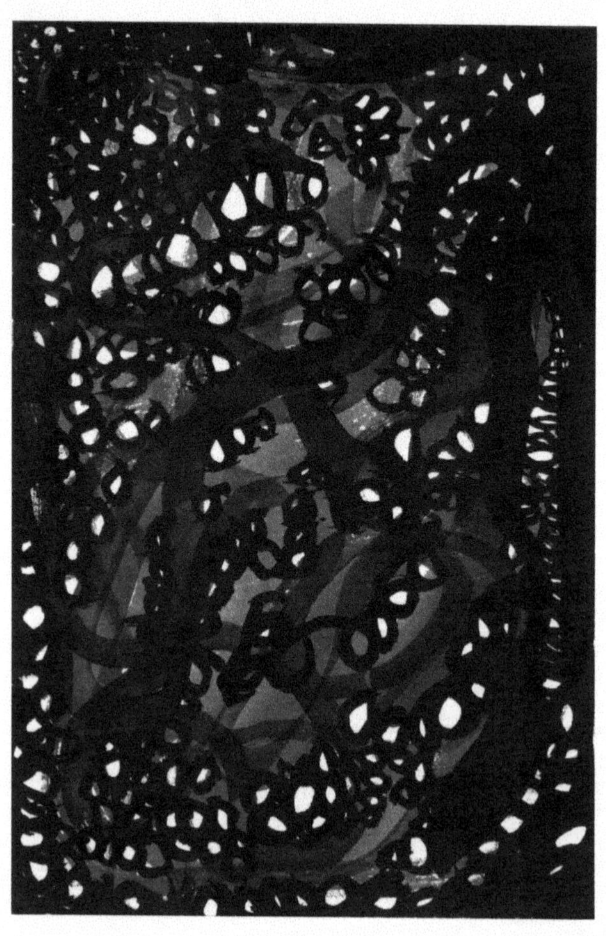

#122: On Thursday night, she went out to see
the same world by moonlight and found, in fast-
traveling clouds, on ice-encrusted marsh, in
brambles and leafless oaks, all interwoven with
deep dark and moon glow, uncountable
shimmerings and expirations, thousands of tiny
voices saying their goodbyes.